Smart Nation

A Blueprint for Modern Armenia

Second Edition

SASSOON GRIGORIAN

Գ

Gomidas Institute
London

ISBN 978-1-909382-83-1

Gomidas Institute
42 Blythe Rd.
London W14 0HA
United Kingdom
www.gomidas.org
info@gomidas.org

To the memory of those men and women
who made the ultimate sacrifice for Artsakh.

CONTENTS

Author's Note

Armenia's economy has advanced considerably since 2016 when the first edition of *Smart Nation* was published. Today, Armenia is approaching an upper middle-class developing economy, Yerevan is becoming as expensive as many European cities, the capital has a vibrancy of café culture, it is becoming more and more connected internationally, its tourism base has broadened widely, roads across the country have improved markedly, government spending is up as is revenue collection, wages have increased but so have costs. Overall, there is an appearance of more affluence, but at what cost?

Armenia is at a critical inflection point where its national security is under constant threat, and its sovereignty questioned by hostile neighbours to its east and west.

Now more than ever, Armenia needs strong policies to help guide it to 2050 and beyond, so it can be more secure and prosperous. The foundations for this future lie in the critical present.

Since 2016, there has been time to reflect and produce a second edition, to recap what has been achieved, what hasn't, and what can still be (see Appendix). Around 70 percent of recommendations and predictions in the first edition have either been adopted in full or in part.

Most unfortunate was the premonition that the Artsakh issue required conflict resolution, not management. That did not eventuate at that time, leading to a lost war and territory for Armenia. As a consequence, Armenia lost its advantageous negotiating position regarding surrounding territories around the Republic of Artsakh. This was something the book warned about.

Despite this, several reforms identified in the first edition of the book have materialised. There are positives but there also remain signs Prime Minister Pashinyan has regrettably reverted to the revisionist doctrine called 'Real Armenia,' and this author proposes replacing it with a 'One Armenia' doctrine. Armenia's negotiating tactics internationally have been woeful, which has angered Russia and pandered to the West. Armenia needs to consider a 360 degree foreign policy as outlined in this book.

A deep shame is the lack of aggressive measures to secure Armenian political leaders imprisoned in Azerbaijan after the 2023 Artsakh invasion.

This book covers many sectors but notable omissions are health and education, given the author's lack of expertise in these areas.

The book aims to be objective and offer concrete recommendations for further developing the Armenian nation. At times, there is criticism, which the author considers justified; it is unavoidable not to have a view on certain critical matters impacting on Armenia.

Armenia's survival has been remarkable, but survival is not enough. It needs to be prosperous, secure, and confident in its identity and position in the world. May it be so.

Foreword

When Sassoon Grigorian approached us ten years ago, he was deeply concerned about Armenia's well-being. Yet he also brought forward a set of recommendations to address those concerns. He outlined opportunities Armenians could consider to change course or accelerate toward a better future. Drawing on his own expertise, his book proved to be practical, innovative, and accessible to a wide audience. It paid particular attention to emerging technologies, while also emphasising social reforms to complement Armenia's positive development.

Now, in this second edition, Grigorian revisits his earlier work with fresh insights and a new set of proposals. His focus has expanded to include artificial intelligence, responsible mining, and human capital. He is mindful of the shifting geopolitical and security landscape around Armenia, and he also addresses pressing social issues such as women's rights, cost-of-living challenges, and well being as vital measures of progress.

Grigorian raises substantial agenda-setting matters for both Armenia and the Armenian diaspora, grounded in the power of shared Armenian human capital. Grigorian is a mover-and-shaker, a high-powered professional, and a public intellectual who deserves our respect and attention.

© 2016 Gomidas Institute

TBILISI

GEORGIA

AZERBAIJAN

Sanahin • Haghbat

Stepanavan •

LORI

TAVUSH

• Ijevan

Gyumri ■   Vanadzor ■   ■ Dilijan

SHIRAK

• Dhovsyunk

Ganja •

Apazan •   Tsaghgasor •

Hrazdan ■   • Charentsavan

Talin •   Mt. Aragats   KOTAYK   Gavar •   Shahumyan •

ARAGATSOTN   Ashtarak ■   Abovyan •

Armavir •   Metsamor •   Gheghard •   Vardenis •   Martakert •

ARMAVIR   Echmiadzin •   YEREVAN ● Geni

KEGHARKUNIK   Kelbajar •   Askeran •   Aghdam •

NAGORNO-KARABAGH (ARTSAKH)

Artashat ■   ARARAT   Jermuk •   STEPANAKERT ● Martuni •

Mt. Ararat Xx   Shushi •

Yegheknadzor ■   Hadrut •   Fuzuli

VAYOTS DZOR   Lachin •   Hoyada

Dogubeyazit •   Sisian •   Qubadli •   Jebrail •

Gorts   SVUNIK   Tatev •

NAKHICHEVAN (AZERBAIJAN)   Kapan ■

TURKEY   Zangelan •

IRAN   Meghri •

KEY

━━━━━ International borders

///// Territorial changes following 1992-1994 Azerbaijani-Armenian War.

•••••••••• Cease-fire line between Artsakh and Azerbaijan until 2020

● Capital cities

■ Locations visited by author

Lake Sevan

ARMENIA

0   25   50

Acronyms

֏, - Armenian Dram (national currency)
ADB - Asian Development Bank
AI – Artificial Intelligence
AWS – Amazon Web Services
CEO – Chief Executive Officer
CEPA – Comprehensive and Enhanced Partnership Agreement
CIA – Counter Intelligence Agency
CIS – Commonwealth of Independent States
CSTO - Collective Security Treaty Organisation
EBRD – European Bank for Reconstruction and Development
ECHR - European Court of Human Rights
EDB – Economic Development Board (Singapore)
EEU – Eurasian Economic Union
EIA – Environmental Impact Assessment
EIB – European Investment Bank
EITI – Extractive Industries Transparency Initiative
EU – European Union
EV – Electric vehicle
FAST – Foundation for Armenian Science and Technology
FDI – Foreign Direct Investment
FIS – Foreign Intelligence Service (Armenia)
G7 – Group of Seven
G20 – Group of Twenty
GCC – Gulf Cooperation Council
GDP – Gross Domestic Product
ICJ - International Court of Justice
ICT – Information Communications and Technology
INSTC – International North-South Transport Corridor
MLRI - Mining Legislation Reform Institute
MNCs – Multinational Companies
NSS – National Security Service (Armenia)
OECD – The Organisation for Economic Cooperation and Development
OSCE - Organisation for Security and Co-operation in Europe
RT – Russia Today

SCO – Shanghai Cooperation Organisation
S20 – Small States of Twenty
SEZ – Special Economic Zone
TRIP - Tourism and Regional Infrastructure Project
TRIPP - Trump Route for International Peace and Prosperity
UAE – United Arab Emirates
UNDP – United Nations Development Programme
UNESCO – United Nations Educational, Scientific, and Cultural Organisation
US – United States
WCIT – World Congress on Innovation and Technology

Smart Nation

A Blueprint for Modern Armenia

Second Edition

Chapter One

Silicon Mountain

"Armenia will develop its first $1 billion startup, not if but when."[1]

This was the prediction a decade ago. Five years later in 2021, Picsart became the first tech unicorn in Armenia.[2]

Armenia's technology sector is the jewel of the crown in Armenia's economy. It is on track to become the largest industry segment.

In 2023, the information technology sector's turnover reached approximately ֏837 billion, marking a 43 percent increase from the previous year,[3] and is the fastest-growing sector in Armenia.

The Armenian government has implemented policies to foster innovation, and the Armenian diaspora has played a crucial role in providing investment and expertise, further propelling the sector's growth. Organisations like the Foundation for Armenian Science and Technology (FAST), Tumo Centre, Granatus Ventures and SmartGateVC provide support for startup development and innovation.

This has resulted in Armenia attracting multinational technology companies, including NVIDIA, Adobe, Cisco, Microsoft, Amazon Web Services (AWS) and Synopsys, establishing a global presence in the industry.

It has also hosted twice the World Congress on Innovation and Technology (WCIT) in Yerevan, underscoring its ambition to become a global tech hub, most recently in 2024. DigiTec, Armenia's largest annual tech event brings together tech leaders, companies and investors, attracting an estimated 40,000 visitors from around the globe. In late 2024, the Armenian ecosystem achieved a major milestone when ServiceTitan, a software platform for home and commercial service businesses, established by Ara Mahdessian and Vahe Kuzoyan, became a publicly listed company, valued around $9 billion at time of listing. Though not founded in Armenia, it has a sizeable presence in Armenia focused on software development, customer support, and research and development.

There are many potential tech unicorns based in Armenia, including SuperAnnotate, an AI data platform founded by brothers Vahan and Tigran Petrosyan. In November 2024, the company secured a $36 million Series B funding round led by Socium Ventures, with participation from NVIDIA.

Another company, Krisp, an AI-powered noise cancellation software company co-founded by Davit Baghdasaryan and Artavazd Minasyan, has garnered significant attention in the technology industry. In February 2021, Krisp raised a total of $17.5 million in funding, including a $9 million Series A extension led by RTP Global, with participation from Storm Ventures.

Having achieved the first prediction, Armenia needs to be bold in providing a vision for the coming decade, and that is to produce the first home grown $10 billion startup.

At the time of writing, this has yet to be formed, though a conducive environment and plan can still be put in place to ensure it becomes reality.

Armenia has a number of organisations to help with its technology roadmap, including FAST, which includes scientists, engineers, and entrepreneurs from around the world. This council collaborates with the Board of Trustees to guide Armenia's science and technology initiatives.

The National Foundation of Science and Advanced Technologies (NFSAT) established in 1997, is a non-profit organisation aimed at developing Armenia's scientific and engineering potential. It provides financial and technological support for scientific research and project development.

The National Centre of Innovation and Entrepreneurship (NCIE) with four branches (Gyumri, Vanadzor, Hrazdan, Kapan) was formed in 2009. The NCIE is a member of the Interstate Council for the Coordination of Scientific and Technical Information (ICCSTI) of the Commonwealth of Independent States (CIS) members. The centre supports the protection and commercialisation of intellectual property and provides support to entrepreneurs.

Tumo is an after-school learning environment where thousands of teenage students are put in charge of their own learning. It is a place where there is access to the Internet and technology. Tumo has facilities in regional areas in Armenia, and has been so successful that its model has been exported to other cities such as Paris, Lyon, Berlin, Mannheim, Beirut, Tirana, Kyiv, and Buenos Aires — with plans for India, Portugal and Spain.

Tumo is well positioned to help train Armenia's young generation in the skills it needs for today's jobs. Tumo has been successful in housing technology companies within its facility in Yerevan, and to have Tumo graduates recruited into such firms. It has a serious advisory body to help in its vision and growth.

Artificial Intelligence: Untapped Opportunity

Artificial Intelligence (AI) is the single largest technology development since the Internet, or world wide web.

AI is a collective term for computer systems that can sense their environment, think, learn, and take action in response to what they sense. AI is used in digital assistants, chatbots, and machine learning models.

AI could contribute up to $15.7 trillion to the global economy in 2030, more than the current industrial output of China and India combined.[4]

AI will continue to impact all aspects of the economy including healthcare: diagnostics, drug discovery, personalised medicine, robotic surgery; finance: fraud detection, algorithmic trading, credit risk assessment; transportation: autonomous vehicles, traffic management, logistics optimisation; education: personalised learning platforms, virtual tutors, automated grading; entertainment: content recommendations, video game AI, generative art; and business:

customer service chatbots, predictive analytics, supply chain optimisation.

It is essentially another layer of infrastructure, like utilities, energy, water, and transport. It is a critical component that impacts every layer of the economy.

No economy or country can afford to be left behind.

From a global point of view, Armenia can and should do much better. According to the 2023 AI Preparedness Index, Armenia ranks 70th among 165 countries.[5] The Index assesses nations' readiness to adopt and implement AI based on set of indicators that cover the countries' digital infrastructure, human capital and labour market policies, innovation and economic integration, and regulation and ethics.

According to the 2024 Global Government Index,[6] Armenia ranks 88th out of 188 governments worldwide. The Index is based on 40 indicators across three pillars including: government; technology sector and data; and infrastructure. If we compare Armenia to other smart small states as a benchmark, Singapore is ranked 2nd; Finland 9th, United Arab Emirates 13th, Denmark 15th, and Israel 17th.

There has been some progress in fostering greater collaboration. The Armenia's Ministry of High-Tech Industry and Mistral AI signed an agreement to foster greater collaboration at the AI Action Summit in Paris in February 2025.[7] Mistral AI is an AI startup from France focused on democratising AI through open-source, efficient, and innovative models, products, and solutions.

The partnership aims to enhance AI infrastructure, support AI driven business solutions, and improve public administration through AI by leveraging Mistral AI's expertise in both commercial and open-source technologies. The partnership is expected to position Armenia as a key player in the regional AI ecosystem, fostering innovation and technological progress.

In July 2025, the Armenian government launched the AI Virtual Institute. This national platform is designed to connect researchers, startups, and technology companies and to position Armenia as a regional hub for excellence in AI. The announcement was made in collaboration with AWS, and Mistral. The Government should consider expanding similar partnerships in the AI field.

In addition, a $500 million public-private partnership with the Government of Armenia, NVIDIA and Firebird.ai (a Yerevan startup) will result in the first AI supercomputing data centre in the Caucasus region.[8] The new investment marks a significant milestone in Armenia's journey toward becoming a leader in next generation technology, building on NVIDIA's existing presence in Armenia.

National AI Plan & Minister for AI

The Armenian government needs to establish a National AI Plan, and a National AI body devoted exclusively to coordinating AI efforts.

A National AI Plan is a comprehensive strategy developed by a government to guide the research, development, deployment, and regulation of AI technologies. These plans outline a country's vision, priorities, and actions to leverage AI for economic growth, innovation, and societal benefits while addressing ethical, legal, and security challenges. To be truly effective, National AI strategies need to be distilled as whole-of-government effort, with action plans and roadmaps that are industry- and sector-specific.

There have been previous calls by the Armenian government to have a National AI Strategy, even as far back as 2021 by then Armenian Deputy Prime Minister, Tigran Avinyan.[9]

Singapore's National AI Strategy, launched in November 2019, aims to position the country as a global leader in AI by integrating it into its economy and society. Its vision is to become a global hub for AI development, deployment, and innovation, leveraging AI to transform the economy and improve the quality of life.

In 2023, it launched the Singapore National AI Strategy 2.0. One of its pillars, which the Armenian government should consider emulating, is having a global outlook for AI. This means connecting to global networks, working with the best, and pooling resources with like-minded organisations to overcome the complex challenges that plague AI today.

As a result, Singapore is a leader in AI readiness, adoption, and usage. By having a strategy and executing against it has meant delivering concrete results: AI is projected to contribute $10 billion to Singapore's economy by 2030; more than 100 AI-focused companies have established since the strategy's launch, including startups and innovation labs; 80 percent of Singapore's public hospitals are using AI to enhance diagnostic accuracy, predict patient outcomes, optimise treatment plans, and reduce healthcare costs by approximately $1 billion over the next decade; an AI-enhanced traffic management system is expected to reduce congestion and improve traffic flow by 10-15 percent; AI integration in logistics has led to 20 percent improvements in operational efficiency for key players; more than 20,000 professionals have trained in AI through government programs.

Other small states that have adopted a National AI plan include the United Arab Emirates (UAE), which focuses on AI adoption in key sectors like healthcare, transportation, and education. Estonia, a digital pioneer in e-government, adopted its National AI Strategy with the aim to integrate AI into governance, business, and society. Luxembourg's AI Strategy focuses on AI for finance, logistics, and space technology, leveraging its strong research institutions and digital infrastructure.

Ideally, a National plan should have a dedicated Minister for AI. The Armenian government has a Minister for High-Tech Industry, and a Deputy Minister, which have responsibility over AI. Having a dedicated Minister for AI could help coordinate between different ministries (eg, education, healthcare, defence) for cohesive AI integration. The UAE was one of the first countries to appoint a Minister for AI, Omar Sultan Al Olama. This role helped accelerate the country's AI Strategy 2031. The position could also be the country's lead representative of the Global AI Summits. The international conference brings together world leaders, policymakers, industry experts, and AI researchers to discuss the future of AI, its governance, and its impact on economies and societies. It serves as a platform for collaboration, innovation, and policy-making.

National Office of AI

There should also be an Office of AI established under the Ministry. Such an office could operate similarly to the European AI Office, which functions as a central hub of AI expertise across EU member states, playing a pivotal role in implementing the AI Act and promoting trustworthy AI development.

The Office is at the centre of AI expertise across the EU. It plays a key role in implementing the AI Act, especially for general purpose AI, fostering the development and use of trustworthy AI, and international cooperation. The Office of AI was established within the European Commission as the centre of AI expertise and forms the foundation for a single European AI governance system.

Within the Office, there are specific units, including excellence in AI and robotics; regulation and compliance; AI safety; AI innovation and policy coordination; AI for societal good; lead scientific advisor; and the advisor for international affairs.

Another model could be the one adopted by the United Kingdom. The Office for AI is responsible for overseeing implementation of the National AI Strategy. The Office is part of the AI Policy Directorate in the Department for Science, Innovation and Technology. Its mission is to drive responsible and innovative uptake of AI technologies for the benefit of everyone in the United Kingdom. Its focus is on three pillars: AI investment; supporting the transition to an AI enabled economy; and AI governance.

Advisory Council on AI

Several national governments have established advisory councils to guide policies and strategies related to AI. The Armenian government should consider the same.

Advisory bodies play crucial roles in shaping national AI policies, ensuring ethical development, promoting the responsible use of AI technologies, and help bring expertise from industry, both local and international.

The United States's National Artificial Intelligence Advisory Committee advises the President and the National AI Initiative Office on matters related to the National AI Initiative, and Canada's

Advisory Council on AI advises the government on building the country's strengths and global leadership, identifying opportunities for economic growth, and ensuring that AI advancements reflect Canadian values.

Singapore's Advisory Council on the Ethical Use of AI and Data advises the Singaporean government on legal, ethical, and policy issues arising from data-driven technologies. This council comprises experts from technology companies, legal fields, and consumer advocacy groups, and its International Advisory Panel on AI consists of leading AI researchers and practitioners who provide strategic advice on research directions, policy, governance, and emerging trends.

Finland's AI Advisory Board supports Finland's mission to position the country as a global leader in AI development and application. The board comprises top-tier experts from research and the corporate sector, providing strategic insights and ensuring high ambition and focus.

UAE's Artificial Intelligence and Advanced Technology Council, guides policies and strategies for research and investments in AI and future technology in Abu Dhabi.

Denmark's National Strategy for AI sets the roadmap for Denmark to be a frontrunner in responsible AI development and use, benefiting individuals, businesses, and society.

These councils and initiatives reflect each country's commitment to fostering responsible AI development and governance, tailored to their unique societal and economic contexts. Armenia would be well placed to establish its own.

AI Education and Skills

Education and skills are critical components in driving any national plan. The previous edition of Smart Nation recommended teaching coding in schools; with the advent of AI, students should be taught to build AI agents. An AI agent is a software-based system that can perceive its environment, process information, and take actions to achieve specific goals. It operates autonomously or semi-autonomously and can continuously learn and adapt based on experience.

This also needs to be applied in terms of AI literacy. Armenia's FAST is piloting an educational program called Generation AI[10] allowing high school students to study advanced mathematics and computer science, with a strong emphasis on python programming and AI fundamentals, coupled with career guidance and mentoring to prepare students for specialised studies and careers in the field.

Governments and businesses need to cultivate a strong pool of AI talent to meet the market's demand for skilled AI professionals that are required in all segments of the economy.

PwC's 2024 AI Jobs Barometer[11] found that sectors with the highest AI penetration were seeing almost a five-fold greater labour productivity growth. Rising labour productivity can generate economic growth, higher wages, and enhanced living standards. Jobs that require AI specialist skills carry up to a 25 percent wage premium in some markets, and growth in jobs that require AI specialist skills has outpaced all jobs since with numbers of AI specialist jobs growing 3 and half times faster than all jobs.

Global AI Action Summit

Armenia should aim to be a future host of the Global AI Action Summit. The Global AI Action Summits have been pivotal in shaping international discourse on AI governance and safety. It began in 2023 in the United Kingdom, and the inaugural summit resulted in the 'Bletchley Declaration', emphasising international cooperation to manage AI challenges and risks.

In the following year, the AI Seoul Summit was hosted by South Korea. Key outcomes included establishing global AI safety standards and fostering collaboration between nations to address AI's ethical and societal implications.

In February 2025, the AI Action Summit was hosted in Paris, France. Key outcomes aimed to broaden AI discussions to include labour market impacts and environmental considerations. A significant outcome was the 'Statement on Inclusive and Sustainable Artificial Intelligence for People and the Planet.'

In 2026 the Summit will be hosted by India. To date, each of the Summit hosts have been G20 economies. There can be a strong argument made that the following host should be a small smart state.

These summits reflect the evolving global landscape of AI, with each host nation contributing to the ongoing dialogue on balancing innovation with ethical considerations and safety standards. It is also an effective means of projecting soft power, as the host plays an influential role in shaping the Summit agenda, as well as projecting its AI capabilities to the globe.

Electric Vehicles (EVs)

Armenia has an opportunity to take advantage of its energy resources, to potentially be a leader in electric vehicle adoption, and subsequently a hub for research and development in its software development. This approach could help in multiple areas. Reduced energy dependence on foreign countries; a cleaner environment, especially in Yerevan, which is experiencing serious pollution levels due to the increased number of vehicles (among other factors); and deepening Armenia's capability as a technology hub.

Electric vehicles represented a small but rapidly growing segment of Armenia's automotive market.

In order to consider electric vehicle adoption, a number of factors need to be taken into account, including affordability, infrastructure, and the country's energy consumption.

Armenia's energy consumption is characterised by a diverse mix of sources, combining domestic production with significant imports. In 2022, primary energy sources included natural gas, primarily from Russia, accounting for approximately 59 percent of the total energy supply.[12] Nuclear energy contributes around 18 percent[13] to Armenia's energy supply, and hydropower accounted for about 30 percent.[14] Renewable energy is a small but growing component of the total overall consumption.

Households are the largest consumers of energy in Armenia, followed by the transportation sector, making up 31.0 percent.[15] This demand is primarily met through imported oil products. It is estimated that transport emissions account for around 22 percent of Armenia's green house gas emissions. Importantly, around 60 percent of Armenia's electricity comes from zero carbon sources, including hydro and nuclear power, making its grid one of the cleanest in the region.[16]

There are other factors that suit Armenia for EV consumption. Armenia's small size and shorter driving distances are well suited for EVs. This reduces range anxiety and makes home or local charging viable even without a large charging network.

Electric vehicles reduce dependence on imported fuel, thus strengthening the trade balance. EV adoption can support green jobs in maintenance, battery logistics, charging infrastructure, and software solutions. Armenia can become a testbed for localised EV solutions in mountainous and cold-weather conditions, useful for regional innovation.

Between 2019-2024 there was a tax exemption for imported EV's to Armenia. In the city of Yerevan, EVs are exempted from paying for vehicle parking. By 2025, 20 percent of public transport in Yerevan was targeted to be fuelled by electricity and hydrogen.[17]

The Government's National Plan for Energy Saving and Renewable Energy, aims to increase EVs by 10 percent (passenger vehicles).[18] With measures to increase EV adoption and usage, it is estimated energy savings in 2030 will reach 36 percent in the transport sector alone.

The government should also consider a dedicated National EV Plan, to continue to take advantage of this technology, reduce pollution and energy dependency, and add value to the sector by providing innovative solutions.

The Armenian government can set public procurement mandates for EV fleets, tap into climate funds (e.g. Green Climate Funds) and green financing. It also needs to continue to expand EV charging across the country, prioritising Yerevan, intercity roads, and border crossings.

One notable factor when it comes to EV vehicles is affordability, with EV's being more expensive than combustion engine vehicles.

Many in Armenia cannot afford this option. EV's depreciate in value when used, and their on-selling is an issue in some markets. Armenia could encourage imports of used EVs from trusted markets like Japan or EU, to address the affordability issue.

Chapter Two

Smart Foreign Affairs

In the first edition of Smart Nation it was mentioned – "*foreign affairs are critical for Armenia, a small nation of three million people, particularly when borders are blockaded on its east and west. Armenia needs a smart foreign policy, one which delicately balances its self-interest against competing interests, while keeping major powers like Russia at bay.*"[19]

Another bold claim. Armenia has no allies, none. It has strong relations with countries like Iran and France, but if Armenia expects a country will enter a war with it if under attack, it will have none. This is a stark reality which needs to be treated very seriously.

In terms of its key multilateral relationships, Armenia's relationship with the European Union is primarily guided by the Comprehensive and Enhanced Partnership Agreement (CEPA), which was signed in 2017 and fully entered into force in March 2021. In 2025, the Parliament approved the first reading of a draft law to launch the country's accession process to the European Union.

Armenia is a member of the Francophonie, and Eurasian Economic Union (EEU), and other members of the EEU include Russia, Belarus, Kazakhstan, and Kyrgyzstan. The EEU promotes economic integration, allowing free movement of goods, services, capital, and labour among member states. In recent years, there have been discussions in Armenia about reassessing its membership due to geopolitical tensions and concerns over economic benefits. Armenia's involvement in key groupings need to be understood in the context of its region, and neighbours, namely Turkey, Azerbaijan, Iran, and Russia.[20]

360 Degree Foreign Policy

Armenia needs to have strong negotiating skills to be able to deliver maximum benefit for itself, and a more nuanced and multilayered policy. Former Ambassador Djerejian has advocated Armenia adopt a 360-degree foreign policy.[21]

A 360-degree foreign policy refers to a comprehensive and holistic approach to international relations, where a nation actively engages with all relevant actors, countries, organisations, and regions— without limiting itself to specific alliances, geographies, or traditional partners. This approach emphasises balance, inclusivity, and adaptability in addressing global challenges and opportunities.

Key pillars include: non-alignment or strategic autonomy, often associated with countries pursuing an independent foreign policy, not tied to specific blocs or power structures; flexibility and adaptability, allows a nation to respond dynamically to changing global circumstances, including economic shifts, conflicts, or emerging technologies; and inclusivity, engages with countries across political ideologies, economic systems, and levels of development, and seeks common ground even with nations that may have differing values or policies.

Some countries which practice this method include India. India often describes its foreign policy as 360 degrees, balancing relations with major powers like the United States, China, Russia, and the EU while strengthening ties with developing nations, particularly in Africa, Latin America, and Southeast Asia. For example, India is part of forums like BRICS (emerging economies Brazil, Russia, China, and South Africa) and the Quad (US, Japan, and Australia).

India has historically had strong relations with Russia, its largest defence supplier since the Cold War. India took a neutral position in relation to the Russia-Ukraine conflict, despite annoyances from Western powers. Despite this, it has expanded its military relations with other countries so it is less dependent from a single supplier. It has a growing defence partnership with the United States, particularly since the 2005 Indo-US Civil Nuclear Agreement; France specially in aviation, with deals for Rafale fighter jets and collaborations in space and maritime security; Israel has become a key supplier of advanced defence technology, including Unmanned Aerial Vehicle's (UAVs) or drones, radars, and missile systems; and Japan with a strong focus on maritime security and joint naval exercises to counterbalance China's influence in the Indo-Pacific.

A small city state like Singapore, which has China to its north, and the fourth most populous country in the globe to its south – Indonesia, needs to have a delicate foreign policy, which consists of preserving sovereignty and independence.

It does this through various methods including: being non-aligned, ensuring that it remains politically independent and not beholden to any major power bloc; advocating for international law, particularly for small states that rely on rules and norms for protection in the global system; effective regional engagement, in Singapore's case this is through Association of South East Asian Nations (ASEAN); engaging in defence diplomacy and having military cooperation agreements with several countries, including hosting training grounds abroad; and employing a hedging strategy, balancing relations between competing major powers (eg., US-China tensions). It emphasises neutrality and refrains from taking sides in great power rivalries while safeguarding its own national interests.

For Armenia, a 360 degree foreign policy is not about being everywhere at once, it's about balancing great power competition, and maximising economic, security, and diplomatic options.

Turkey: Diplomatic Crossroads

Since the first edition of Smart Nation, much has occurred between relations between Armenia and Turkey.

One of the key developments has included Turkey's active involvement in the Nagorno-Karabagh conflict, and providing overt military assistance to Azerbaijan, both in arms and through personnel.

To recap, Armenia and Turkey have no formal diplomatic relations, and the border between both countries has been closed since 1993.

In 2009 Turkey and Armenia signed protocols which intended to set a path of normalisation between the two countries.

The intent of the protocols was positive, justified, and necessary. Its execution was hopelessly poor and some of the content controversial. The deal followed more than one year of talks. It was designed to allow the opening of borders and to set up a formal diplomatic relationship.

Then, at the time, Turkey decided to suspend the ratification process after the Turkish Prime Minister Recep Tayyip Erdogan announced that Turkish ratification depended on a peace deal in the Nagorno-Karabagh conflict. On the same day, President Sargsyan suspended Armenia's ratification process whilst announcing Armenia's intent to pursue the process of normalisation with Turkey.

The protocols failed for a number of reasons. First, the benefits of open borders was not clearly explained, particularly in economic terms. Second, both countries carry significant historical baggage, not least Turkey's non-recognition and denial of the 1915 Armenian Genocide. These events continue to create deep mistrust.

After Armenia's 2018 Velvet Revolution, Prime Minister Nikol Pashinyan signalled a willingness to engage with Turkey without preconditions. Turkey remained firm in its support for Azerbaijan and called for the return of 'occupied territories' in Nagorno-Karabagh.

During the 2020 Artsakh war (Artsakh is the Armenian name for Nagorno-Karabagh), Turkey provided significant military and political support to Azerbaijan. Relations deteriorated further, as Armenia accused Turkey of direct involvement.

This took a turn in December 2021, when Armenia appointed Ruben Rubinyan, Deputy Speaker of the National Assembly as special envoy for Armenia-Turkey relations. A recommendation made in the first edition of Smart Nation in 2016. Turkey named Serdar Kılıç, a former ambassador to the US, as its envoy.

The first direct talks took place in January 2022 in Moscow, aiming for normalisation without preconditions. In July 2022, both sides agreed to reopen the land border for third-country nationals; and launch direct air cargo trade. Flights between Yerevan and Istanbul resumed in early 2022.

In July 2024, envoys met at the Alican-Margara border crossing — the first meeting at the actual border. They discussed reopening the Akyaka-Akhurik railway and simplifying visa procedures, and both reaffirmed their commitment to normalise relations gradually and pragmatically.

In recent years, the border at the Margara checkpoint has been opened for the delivery of humanitarian aid, first for victims of the Turkish earthquake in February 2023, and then aid to Syria, and open for ten days.[22]

Armenia and Turkey have been in discussions regarding the restoration of the 10-11th century Ani bridge across the Akhurian River, which once connected to the Silk Road. The bridge is symbolic because it connects present day Turkey and the city of Ani with Armenia. This would be a significant symbolic gesture if realised.

Another recommendation in the first edition of Smart Nation, which has since been implemented was for Armenia to commission an independent report into the economic benefits of open borders between Armenia and Turkey. The Armenian government commissioned a study by Berlin Economics[23] to evaluate the potential trade impact of reopening the Armenia–Turkey border.

Key findings included, if the Armenian-Turkish border had opened in 2021, Turkey would have accounted for 12 percent of Armenia's total foreign trade. In reality, Armenia's trade with Turkey in 2021 amounted to only 1 percent of the total.

At the same time, the opening of the border would lead to a change in Armenia's trade structure: the EU would become the leading country (20 percent of trade), followed by Russia (14 percent) and Turkey (12 percent), while currently the top three are Russia (32 percent), the EU (18 percent) and China (15 percent).

Most of the exports from Armenia to Turkey would consist of stones, glass, jewellery ($51 million per year), food, beverages, tobacco ($47 million per year), and minerals, including ore ($19 million per year). Armenia's potential exports to Turkey in 2021 could have amounted to $185 million, equal to 6.7 percent of its total exports in that year.

Potential imports from Turkey to Armenia could have made $678 million in 2021, equivalent to 12.8 percent of Armenia's total imports in that year. The main trade items could have been machinery and equipment ($142 million), textiles and clothing ($139 million), and chemicals, including medicines ($68 million).

The opening of the border may affect local companies in different ways: some would benefit and some would not, but overall the decision would bring more benefits to the country's economy.

An area that would require further analysis by the Armenian government on the economic benefits is jobs, where they would be created, and their impact; as well as how the border opening would impact on Armenia's regional areas such as Gyumri, as well as Turkey's eastern towns and cities, where a significant part of the population is Kurdish, who overall have poorer economic living conditions. This is strategically important in considering the economic impact of the border opening. These are many other areas which should be considered as part of the normalisation process.

As stated in the first edition of Smart Nation *"the opening of borders between the two countries needs to be in response to a movement that comes from both peoples, not stipulated or forced by powerful third parties, such as the United States or other countries."*

In August 2025, former member of the Turkish Parliament, Garo Paylan, who is also of Armenian heritage, called on Turkish President Recep Tayyip Erdoğan to open the Armenia–Turkey border, given one of the previous preconditions was an end to the Nagorno-Karabagh conflict.[24]

To do that, there needs to be greater effort to establish direct links between both countries. For example, a direct path from Yerevan to Doğubayazıt, located in Turkey's southeast, and at the foot of Mount Ararat, is only 80 kilometres. To drive that same distance now is 640 kilometres because travellers have to cross north into Georgia, then to Turkey and drive back south.

Also reactivating the Kars-Gyumri railway. Kars is located in Turkey's east, and Gyumri (formerly known as Leninakan) is located in Armenia's northwest. Originally completed in 1899, the railway was highly important during the Soviet era, as the only direct rail link between Turkey and the Soviet Union. The Kars-Gyumri section has not been operational since 1993.

A smart foreign affairs policy would seek to establish a bilateral agreement for road transportation with Turkey, modelled on the flight agreement between the two countries. This would not only enable trade, but also revitalise tourism between the countries. The potential of tourism, particularly for Turkey's east, is an untapped opportunity.

Serious consideration should be given to think of new ways to break the deadlock on the border. Creating a framework such as a 'special visa free zone' could be considered. This area could cover the historic city of Ani bordering on both countries, and Mount Ararat, Armenia's national symbol, currently in Turkey. Kharkov, an Armenian village located right on the border and overlooking Ani, can only be accessed through prior permission or approved travel groups. This burdensome process needs to be simplified.

A special zone could be designated around these areas and allow citizens of Armenia and travellers from there to cross and visit the site without formal approvals. Currently both Armenia and Turkey offer visa on arrival from citizens from those respective countries.

In order to do this though, there needs to be a climate of trust. Turkey is provocatively converting the historic Armenian Cathedral of Ani, also known as Sourp Asdvadzadzin (Holy Mother of God), into a mosque.[25] The cathedral, a UNESCO World Heritage site located in Kars Province, represents one of the most significant examples of medieval Armenian architecture and the spiritual heart of the former Armenian Kingdom of Ani. Any frameworks established need to recognise this fact.

A transport corridor could also be established around Mount Ararat linking to Armenia, which could help facilitate trade. Mount Ararat currently hosts a Turkish military facility, sometimes is blocked to travellers due to security tensions. This could complicate such a proposal. If both Turkey and Armenia could agree, it would signal a major step of improved relations between both countries.

For Turkey, it would generate significant tourist traffic and revenue from historical sites; for travellers from Armenia, it would make travel to these sites much more convenient and efficient. Above all, it would end a deadlock. It needs to be done in a climate of trust, and recognising and preserving Armenian sites, not converting them to Islamic ones.

Iran – The Strategic Partner

Iran is one of the most strategic and important relations for Armenia. It is the only country that has steadfastly and publicly declared any proposed changes to borders it shares with Armenia's Syunik province could lead to their military intervention.[26]

Iran has declared that any change to the borders in the region is unacceptable, in reference to the proposed 'Zangezur Corridor' through Armenia's Syunik province, a claim Azerbaijan has made to access Armenia's southern corridor to provide a direction connection to its exclave in Nakhichevan, which is separated from Azerbaijan, no more than 40 kilometres.

Iran is the only country that has overtly and, on many occasions, declared it will abandon its policy of restraint and neutrality and engage in countermeasures if Azerbaijan decides to change international borders, which it shares.

One should not be naïve. Iran and Armenia share mutual interests that the borders remain as they are. The large presence of ethnic Azeris in Iran has meant Iran is very conscious not to have a strong and influential Azerbaijan, as that could destabilise internal politics in Iran.

The northern region of Iran is comprised of an Azeri minority, the country's largest ethnic group after Persians, comprising an estimated 15 to 20 million people, primarily residing in northwestern provinces such as East Azerbaijan, West Azerbaijan, Ardabil, and Zanjan. While they are predominantly Shia Muslims, like the majority of Iranians, they maintain a distinct cultural identity. Azeris have historically held significant roles in Iran's political, military, and economic life, including Iran's current President Masoud Pezeshkian.

For many years Iran was a lifeline to Armenia, particularly during the first Nagorno-Karabagh conflict, when the borders of Turkey and Azerbaijan was closed and Georgia unstable.

The Armenian diaspora in Iran is one of the oldest Armenian diaspora communities in the world (other than Jerusalem). Iran's

Armenian community emerged when Shah Abbas, ruler of the Safavid dynasty, relocated hundreds of thousands of Armenians from Nakhichevan, in the 17th century.

Iran is a significant economy and has the world's second largest energy supply, which unfortunately for Armenia, the latter has not been able to leverage due to its existing energy supplies from Russia. Armenia is unable to extradite itself from this state of affairs – not to mention complications related to sanctions applied to countries like Iran.

Armenia needs to augment its energy supply and reliance, given it has options. Armenia imports approximately 87.5 percent of its natural gas from Russia, primarily through Gazprom Armenia, a subsidiary of Russia's Gazprom,[27] and around 70 percent of petroleum oils.[28]

Armenia is actively seeking to diversify its energy sources, including expanding renewable energy projects, enhancing energy efficiency measures, strengthening energy cooperation with Iran, and extending the gas-for-electricity swap agreement until at least 2030.

The Armenia–Iran gas-for-electricity swap agreement is a strategic bilateral deal that allows Iran to export natural gas to Armenia, and in return, Armenia exports electricity to Iran. It's been in place since 2009. How it works is Iran supplies Armenia with natural gas via the Iran-Armenia gas pipeline, and Armenia uses the gas to generate electricity at its thermal power plants. Armenia then sends three kilowatt-hours of electricity back to Iran for every one cubic meter of gas it receives.

There are many opportunities that could be pursued to strengthen economic and trade relations.

As mentioned in Smart Nation first edition, a trading corridor which has not been considered is the route between Armenia and Iran through Azerbaijan's exclave of Nakhichevan, located to Armenia's south, geographically separate from the main part of Azerbaijan. If this transport corridor were available, it would significantly reduce travel times to Iran, one of Armenia's largest export and import markets. The current corridor involves going through mountainous terrain through Armenia's southern Syunik province.

Another recommendation that was mentioned in the first edition of this book was the establishment of a Special Economic Zone (SEZ) along the Armenian and Iranian border. These zones are a designated geographic area within a country where business and trade laws are more liberal than in the rest of the country. These zones are created to attract foreign investment, boost exports, and stimulate economic activity.

To the Armenian government's credit at the time, in 2017, the Meghri Free Economic Zone was established in Meghri, Syunik Province, right on the border with Iran. Its purpose is to facilitate trade and serve as a regional hub for logistics, processing, and export. At the time of the launch, the free economic zone was expected to attract $350-400 million in investment.[29]

It attracts foreign direct investment, especially in light industry, food processing, pharmaceuticals, electronics, and logistics. Advantages for investors includes no customs duties, no Value Added Tax (VAT), profit tax, or property tax for resident companies, simplified licensing and regulatory procedures, and full foreign ownership permitted, thus enhancing Armenia's position as a gateway between Iran and Europe and Russia.

Several Armenian and Iranian companies have launched small-scale agricultural-processing initiatives, such as dry fruit production, pomegranate juice processing, and organic herbal teas and extract. These projects take advantage of Meghri's unique subtropical microclimate.

Another area to strengthen relations is through tourism. It was estimated that around 154,000 Iranian tourists visited Armenia during 2024.[30]

Iran consistently ranks among the top three countries of origin for tourists to Armenia, alongside Russia and Georgia. The influx of Iranian visitors is particularly notable during Nowruz (Iranian New Year in March), a peak travel period, and Vardavar – Armenia's water festival where everyone, no matter the circumstance, can be doused with water. This joyous festival which originated during pagan times is associated with the goddess Astghik, the goddess of water and fertility. Iranian tourists are noticeable, celebrating with their dancing and singing.

The sustained interest from Iranian tourists is attributed to factors such as visa-free travel, cultural and religious ties, proximity, and Armenia's reputation as a safe and welcoming destination.

Furthermore, many Iranians visit Armenia, not only for the freedom they enjoy; they also attend concerts performed by international Iranians in Armenia (because they are not permitted to perform in Iran), and many Iranians apply for visas in the US Embassy in Armenia (as Iran does not have a US embassy).

Some Iranians travel for dental work, cosmetic surgery, or other private healthcare services.

In August 2025, Armenian Prime Minister Nikol Pashinyan and Iranian President Masoud Pezeshkian signed a joint declaration at the Armenia-Iran Business Forum. The declaration planned to increase bilateral trade to $3 billion (currently $748 million), implement a standard certification systems helping cross border trade, the building of a second Arax River bridge, and reaffirming their commitment to strengthening their strategic partnership.

To further strengthen bilateral relations, additional investment is required to boost tourism from Iran. These could include expanding direct flights between Yerevan and key Iranian cities such as Tehran, Tabriz, Isfahan, Mashhad; upgrade border infrastructure at the Meghri–Nurduz crossing to reduce waiting times; improve road conditions from the Iranian border to Yerevan and tourist areas; and launch special Nowruz and Vardavar festival packages with cultural performances, food, and guided tours. Armenia also has the advantage of providing Persian speaking services to tourists, given an Armenian population from Iran now residing in Armenia.

As a landlocked country, access to ports and sea routes is important. Iran has allowed Armenia to get access to its ports of Chabahar and Bandar Abbas to facilitate trade with India.[31]

To support this initiative, Armenia approved a $200 million loan to construct a tunnel along its border with Iran.[32] This infrastructure project is designed to connect Armenia directly to Iranian ports, particularly Chabahar, enhancing its role in the International North-

South Transport Corridor (INSTC) and providing an alternative trade route that bypasses traditional corridors through Turkey and Azerbaijan.

Currently most Armenian goods transit through Georgia's Black Sea ports (like Poti and Batumi), which creates a single-point vulnerability – any disruption (political, economic, or environmental) in Georgia directly affects Armenia's trade.

Access to the Persian Gulf through Iran with ports like Chabahar and Bandar Abbas offer Armenia access to the Indian Ocean trade routes, linking it with India, the Gulf, East Africa, and Southeast Asia, an alternative to relying solely on northern routes through Russia and Europe.

The transport corridor between Armenia and Iran, namely through Syunik province, is critical. Work continues on improving roads in Syunik linking to Iran.

Another untapped area that requires further exploration is the potential role Armenia can play as a 'honest broker' between Iran and western nations who consistently apply sanctions on Iran. Armenia is one of few countries that has strong relations with Iran, while also having stable relations with the EU and other western States. This is a real opportunity to engage an experienced Armenian diplomat, who may have worked previously in one of these western countries and is familiar with the geopolitical situation of the area to be undertake this task. The Armenian government could consider appointing a Special Envoy for this role.

Other examples where small states have acted as 'honest brokers' include Qatar, who have long facilitated ceasefires, hostage exchanges, and humanitarian negotiations between Israel, and Hamas. Qatar also played a role to help neutralise the conflict between Iran and Israel during 2025. Similar to Armenia, Qatar has a population of around three million people, only 13 percent Qatari. Diplomacy is central to how Qatar sees itself. Its constitution explicitly states that Qatari foreign policy is based on the principle of strengthening international peace and security by means of encouraging peaceful resolution of international disputes.[33]

Playing the role of 'honest broker' could help further strength Iran-Armenia ties, as well as strengthen Armenia's position as a valuable and trusted partner in the region.

Russia – The Case for Recalibration

Of all of Armenia's bilateral relations, the most monumental shift in the last decade has come with its relations with Russia, which requires a significant recalibration.

A decade ago, Armenia would have faced criticism for caving in to major powers, primarily Russia. Now, it faces criticism for potentially stoking the Russian bear.

Russia had been an important ally for Armenia since the early 19th century. The two countries' historic relationship has its roots in the 1826–28 war between the Russian empire and the Persian empire after which Eastern Armenia was ceded to Russia. Moreover, Russia was often considered a protector of the Christian subjects of the Ottoman empire, including the Armenians.

After the dissolution of the Soviet Union, Armenia had been regarded as the only ally of Russia among the three Caucasus nations, which also include Georgia and Azerbaijan.

One of the major developments since the first edition of this book is Armenia effectively freezing its membership to the Collective Security Treaty Organisation (CSTO). The CSTO is a Russia-led intergovernmental military alliance formed in 2002, at the time comprising six post-Soviet states: Armenia, Belarus, Kazakhstan, Kyrgyzstan, Russia, and Tajikistan. Its primary objective is to ensure collective defence and security among member nations.

In February 2024, Armenia's Prime Minister, Nikol Pashinyan, confirmed that Armenia had frozen its participation in the CSTO. In December 2024, he stated that Armenia considered itself outside the CSTO and had crossed the point of no return regarding its membership status. In March 2025, Armenia officially notified the CSTO that it would not participate in its financing.

The withdrawal was a culmination of growing dissatisfaction with the CSTO, particularly due to the organisation's inaction during Armenia's conflicts with Azerbaijan.

Armenia remains a member of the Eurasian Economic Union (EEU). It officially joined the EEU on January 2, 2015, following the signing of the accession treaty on October 9, 2014. The EEU is an economic union comprising Armenia, Belarus, Kazakhstan, Kyrgyzstan, and Russia, aiming to facilitate the free movement of goods, services, capital, and labour among member states.

Despite its membership in the EEU, Armenia has been strengthening its ties with the European Union (EU). In 2017, Armenia signed the Comprehensive and Enhanced Partnership Agreement (CEPA) with the EU, which entered into force in 2021. More recently, in March 2025, Armenia passed a law initiating the process for eventual EU membership. These moves have led to tensions with Russia, as officials have warned that pursuing EU membership is incompatible with continued participation in the EEU.

The EEU is largely seen as Russia's alternative to the EU, a political and economic union of states in Europe. The Union is represented by Nursultan Nazarbayev, President of Kazakhstan since 1991; Alexander Lukashenko, President of Belarus since 1994; and Vladimir Putin, President or Prime Minister since 1999. The EEU consists of countries that lack democracy and transparency.

Further, the Russian 102nd military base remains operational in Gyumri, Armenia. Established in the 1990's, this base is a significant component of Russia's military presence in the South Caucasus. Under a bilateral agreement extended in 2010, the base is authorised to operate until 2044, with provisions for automatic five-year extensions thereafter.

At the same time in an effort to stamp its sovereignty, there has been a steady withdrawal of Russian border troops on Armenia's borders. As of 1 January 2025, Russian border guards withdrew from the Armenia-Iran border.[34] As of 1 March 2025, Russian border guards ceased operations at the Margara checkpoint on the Armenia–Turkey border, with Armenian border guards now solely responsible for this crossing.[35]

The reality is, whether Armenia likes it or not, it still has a dependence on Russia in several facets. Whether it be natural gas, nuclear fuel, wheat imports, or other areas, it cannot overlook these critical dependencies. It cannot take a binary foreign policy approach, be it aligning with one foreign power or another, it needs to be balanced and 360 degrees.

Armenia's geopolitical position is complex. While seeking to assert greater autonomy and diversify its international partnerships, Armenia must carefully navigate its existing dependencies on Russia. A nuanced foreign policy that balances these factors without compromising its economic and security interests. The last point is essential – security interests.

There must be focus on shared interests, rather than reacting when interests diverge. Russia is not an ally. It is a cunning and ruthless operator dealing with countries for its strategic interest. But it wields enormous influence on security issues in the region. Deteriorating relations cannot be at the cost of Armenia's security interests.

The Armenian government must better leverage the Armenian diaspora within the Russian Federation estimated to be a community of around two million people. There are many cohorts, including those who emigrated from Armenia after independence, Armenians working in Russia, and an older community going back generations. But rather than leverage the community, the Armenian government has attracted criticism from these circles for deteriorating relations and the handling of the Artsakh conflict. These criticisms have included Union of Armenians of Russia, led by Ara Abramyan;[36] Editor in Chief of Russia Today (RT) media, Margarita Simonyan;[37] and unsurprisingly, Russia's foreign Minister Sergey Lavrov who has Armenian heritage from his father's side.

And although these figures are criticised for taking the Russian narrative and position, it is undeniable that those with Armenian heritage hold positions of considerable influence within the Russian government and state apparatus, like no other Armenian diasporan community. Whether it be Foreign Minister Lavrov; Russian State media through Marita Simonyan and Armen Oganesyan, CEO of Voice of Russia, Roman Babayan, a prominent television host; or cultural policy like Karen Shakhnazarov, Director-General, Mosfilm (stateowned film studio), who is a descendant of the famous Melik-Shahnazarian princely family from Nagorno-Karabagh.

Now more than ever, there must be focus on mutual security interests. For example, both countries wish to prevent the spread of terrorist and extremist groups from the Middle East into the Caucasus; neither wish to have a dominant nor assertive Turkey in the region; and Russia has an interest in having a unified air defence system for the Commonwealth of Independent States (CIS), which Armenia is part of.

The course correct for recalibration starts with mutual interest. Armenia needs to strategically dissect these with Russia, utilising all means at its disposal, for its benefit.

India – Emerging Partner

Armenia must expand its diplomatic and economic horizons beyond traditional power centres. Among the emerging partners that offer both opportunity and alignment of interest, India stands as a compelling partner. With shared civilizational depth, democratic institutions, and a common interest in regional stability and connectivity, Armenia and India are quietly constructing a partnership that may become pivotal in a multipolar Eurasia.

Armenia's ties with India are rooted in centuries of cultural exchange and trade. Armenian merchants were once embedded in the commercial fabric of Mughal India, establishing vibrant communities in cities like Agra, Surat, and Madras. Armenian churches still stand in Kolkata and Chennai as monuments to this forgotten legacy, and dotted across the country. In the 18th century, Armenian intellectuals in Madras were among the first to articulate the vision of Armenian self-determination, long before the modern independence movement had taken form. Despite this shared past, the relationship between Armenia and India remained largely dormant, until recently.

Since Armenia's independence, bilateral relations with India have gained momentum. India has emerged as a supplier of advanced military equipment to Armenia, including radar systems and rocket artillery, marking a break from Armenia's near-total dependency on Russian defence exports. These reflect a growing strategic trust.

Diplomatically, India has expressed consistent support for a peaceful conflict resolution in the South Caucasus, including the sovereignty of Armenia. Yerevan has reciprocated by backing India's territorial integrity in Kashmir and has supported India's positions in multilateral forums. Educational exchanges have also grown, with increasing numbers of Armenian students attending Indian universities and vice-a-versa, particularly in the fields of medicine and engineering.

Armenia must proactively position itself as a key node in the International North-South Transport Corridor (INSTC)—a trade route connecting India to Europe through Iran, Armenia, and Georgia. As mentioned earlier, Iranian ports such as Chabahar and Bandar Abbas can serve as Armenia's gateway to the Indian Ocean.

A dedicated Armenia–India economic cooperation framework should be negotiated, with a focus on key sectors. The creation of a bilateral business council and an annual strategic dialogue between Minister of Foreign Affairs and defence would ensure continuity and ambition in this evolving partnership.

Another area for consideration is the formation of a strategic counsel modelled on the Quad. The Quad, short for the Quadrilateral Security Dialogue, is a strategic forum comprising Japan, the United States, India, and Australia. It is not a formal military alliance, but a partnership focused on promoting a free, open, and inclusive Indo-Pacific region. The leaders of these countries meet on a regular basis focusing on key pillars. Some have argued it is considered a counter weight to China in the region.

Given India's experience, there is also an opportunity to create a trilateral working group with Iran, India, and Armenia to explore strategic logistics cooperation.

India's strength in digital public infrastructure and scalable education technologies can help Armenia modernise its institutions. Partnering with Indian universities and think tanks on research, vocational training, and startup incubation can stimulate Armenia's human capital development, especially in areas like AI, cybersecurity, biotech, and space technologies.

India's success with its digital identity initiative Aadhaar and digital governance offers a blueprint for Armenia's own e-government and citizen services roadmap. Aadhaar is India's national biometric digital identity system, and it is one of the largest and most ambitious identity projects in the world. It is essentially a 12-digit unique identification number issued to Indian residents by the Unique Identification Authority of India.

It is based on the individual's biometric (fingerprints, iris scan) and demographic information (name, date of birth, address, etc). Enrolment is voluntary, but Aadhaar is widely used for government services and private sector verification. This initiative has resulted in improved service delivery and reduced fraud/leakages in welfare programs; enabled financial inclusion; and supported India's shift to a digital economy, including e-KYC and online authentication.

It is worth noting that Armenia's Information Systems Agency of Armenia has made strides in digital governance in recent years including the first national public service gateway for Armenia, called Hartak.[38] Hartak is a one-stop online platform that centralises access to public services and life event guidance for citizens, residents, and diasporan Armenians relocating to Armenia.

United States: The Delicate Balance

The United States has an active role in Armenian affairs, partly due to an active Armenian-American community. The United States government has historically provided significant aid to Armenia, which is considered to receive one of the highest amounts of aid per capita from the United States in the world. According to the Department of State, the United States has invested approximately $3.3 billion in Armenia to support democratic reforms, economic growth and resilience, and humanitarian assistance.[39]

Armenia's relationship with the United States is complicated by the very good relations the United States has with Turkey and Azerbaijan, both of whom blockade the border with Armenia. As well United States' rivalry with Russia, and Iran.

One fact that is often ignored is the roots of US–Armenia relations trace back to the early 20th century, marked by American humanitarian assistance during the Armenian Genocide and President Woodrow Wilson's advocacy for Armenian self-determination. Following Armenia's independence from the Soviet Union in 1991, the United States swiftly recognised the new republic and established diplomatic relations.

In January 2025, Armenia and the United States signed a Strategic Partnership agreement, signalling a deepening of bilateral cooperation across various sectors, including defence, economy, and democratic governance. This move reflected a pivot, given that Armenia has been distancing from the Russian-led framework like the CSTO.

However, Armenia must proceed with caution. Put simply, the United States, nor any other country, cannot guarantee Armenia's security. There are two key moments in recent history that should be etched in US-Armenia foreign relations.

Firstly, no one should ever forget how, in September 2023, Yuri Kim, who served as the Acting Assistant Secretary of State for European and Eurasian Affairs, Department of State testified before Congress just days before Azerbaijan's military offensive in Nagorno-Karabagh,[40] and stated unequivocally, *"we will not tolerate any military action. We will not tolerate any attack on the people of Nagorno-Karabagh. That is very clear."*

Not only was military action tolerated, it occurred unimpeded under its very noses.

Second, in late September 2023, following Azerbaijan's military offensive in Nagorno-Karabagh, then USAID Administrator Samantha Power visited Armenia to address the humanitarian crisis affecting displaced Armenians. During her visit, Power announced that the United States would provide $11.5 million in humanitarian assistance to support those affected by the conflict.[41] This aid was intended to cover essential needs, including food, social support, and efforts to reunite families separated during the hostilities. In other words, $115 each for the estimated 100,000 displaced persons. When asked whether she agreed with warnings from Armenia's Prime Minister Nikol Pashinyan that the exodus reflected 'ethnic cleansing,' Power, a former genocide scholar, declined to use the term.[42]

This episode demonstrated the cold hard facts of real politics. States will act in their own interest. The United States has demonstrated its strong interest in supporting Armenia's democratic governance reforms through financial assistance, strategic partnerships, and targeted programs aimed at strengthening institutions, promoting transparency, and empowering civil society, less so its national security.

In July 2025, a proposal was floated by the US ambassador to Turkey, Thomas Barrack that an American company have a long term lease on the proposed transport corridor to Nakhichevan through Armenia's strategic Syunik region, as a means of brokering a peace deal between Armenia and Azerbaijan – a proposal that was rejected by the Armenian government at the time.[43] Then, in an apparent reversal in the following month, it was accepted as part of a declaration of peace signed by Armenia and Azerbaijan in the United States. Such an initiative does not serve Armenia's interests but only US interests, which can change at any time at its choosing.

The United States has partnered with the Armenian government to fight institutional corruption, improve e-governance, strengthen electoral and political processes, and foster a strong civil society and independent media. These efforts are part of a broader strategy to enhance Armenia's democratic institutions and promote the rule of law.[44] These are also US interests.

There is a significant opportunity to improve technology ties. One small step was made in August 2025, when the United States and Armenia signed a Memorandum of Understanding on AI and semiconductor innovation partnership which seeks to deepen collaboration and cooperation.[45]

For Armenia, its interest in the United States should be focused more on attracting investment in the Armenian technology sector. The United States is the largest global investor in technology, research and development, venture capital investments, and strategic infrastructure funding. As the technology sector becomes one of Armenia's highest growing sectors, and increasingly more important in its economy, it is this sphere that Armenia should deepen its relationship with the United States.

China: The Silk Road Reimagined

China was among the first nations to recognise Armenia's independence in 1991, setting the stage for a series of bilateral agreements that would shape their relationship. The 'Agreement on the Basics of Trade and Economic Cooperation' signed in January 1992 laid the groundwork for economic collaboration. Over the years, approximately 70 agreements, protocols, and memoranda have been signed, encompassing areas such as agriculture, education, culture, and technical-economic cooperation.[46]

In 2024, bilateral trade reached $2.8 billion, marking a 34 percent increase from the previous year. This surge positions China as Armenia's third-largest trading partner. Armenia primarily exports copper and other ores to China, while importing a diverse array of goods, including machinery, electronics, and textiles.[47] Armenia imports significantly more than it exports. Efforts are underway to address this disparity, focusing on enhancing Armenia's export capabilities and attracting Chinese investments in sectors like agriculture and technology.

Beyond economics, Armenia and China have fostered cultural and educational ties. Initiatives include the establishment of Chinese language schools in Armenia and collaborative research projects. These exchanges not only enhance mutual understanding but also lay the foundation for deeper, long-term cooperation.

As stated in the first edition of Smart Nation, one might wonder what interest the Chinese have regarding relations with Armenia. One of the reasons is China's Xinjiang Uyghur Autonomous Region, in China's northwest. It is the largest Chinese administrative division, and contains many Uyghurs, members of a Turkic ethnic group. Tensions continue with the Chinese government and Uyghurs seeking more autonomy.

Both Turkey and Azerbaijan, Armenia's neighbours and themselves with majority Turkic populations, support Uyghurs' claim for increased autonomy. Therefore, it is in China's interests to have strong relations in the Caucasus that balance that view.

That said, Armenia's former ambassador to China, Sergey Manasaryan, has said there has been a stagnation in Armenian-

Chinese relations stemming from Armenia's low level of relations with Russia.[48]

Armenia has not shown much interest in China's 'Belt and Road' initiative, despite high-level commitments. This ambitious project was launched in 2013, a global infrastructure and economic development strategy aimed at enhancing regional connectivity and fostering economic cooperation across Asia, Europe, Africa, and beyond, inspired by the ancient Silk Road trade routes.

Armenia still holds formal membership in the inactive Religious Freedom Alliance, which should not be confused with the International Religious Freedom Summit. Founded by former US Secretary of State Mike Pompeo as a counter-China initiative, the alliance has been dormant. Despite that, Armenia remains a member of this informal alliance.

Unlike in Georgia and Azerbaijan, where China has made regionally significant investments, its economic footprint in Armenia remains modest. China-Armenia relations are focused on soft power, namely cultural and economic related.

In 2018, the healthcare system received 200 ambulances from China. China also provided support during the Covid-19 pandemic. In 2021, with the assistance of the Chinese government, Yerevan received 100,000 doses of the Sinovac vaccine. Subsequently, the Chinese helped Armenia procure 1.2 million doses of the Sinopharm vaccine. Yerevan's bus fleet has been supplemented by approximately 250 buses. Along with them, spare parts for maintenance and repair were also delivered to Armenia.[49]

In 2025, Armenia and China elevated their bilateral relationship by formally establishing a strategic partnership. This was announced during a meeting between Chinese President Xi Jinping and Armenian Prime Minister Nikol Pashinyan on the sidelines of the Shanghai Cooperation Organisation (SCO) Summit in Tianjin.[50] The Summit is focused on regional security and Armenia is a dialogue partner. China also indicated its support for Armenia's potential future accession to the SCO.

As part of a 360 degree foreign policy, Armenia needs to deepen its relations with China to a more strategic level, such as broadening military ties, as well as attracting investment from Chinese companies into Armenia's technology sector. Armenia ought to have the strongest relations with China in the Caucasus – and that is currently not the case.

Georgia: Unnatural Rival

If there is a nation that Armenia should have good relations with, it is its northern neighbour Georgia. The two have much in common: Christian nations neighbouring Muslim countries (Turkey and Azerbaijan); Armenians constitute one of the largest minority populations in Georgia, occupying many positions of influence; the Armenian priest Mesrop Mashtots is believed to have invented the Georgian alphabet in the 5th century (he also invented the Armenian alphabet); and living together side by side for many centuries.

Despite the similarities, relations between the two countries are not as good as they could or should be. Georgia is burdened by its own challenges. It has separatist movements within its borders, including Abkhazia and South Ossetia (both territories recognised by Russia as independent), as well as Ajaria. Armenia has not recognised South Ossetia and Abkhazia as independent states.

Georgia's province of Samtskhe-Javakheti, located in the nation's south-west, is majority Armenian. Local Armenians have been advocating improved recognition of their rights. These include campaigning against appropriation of Armenian churches by the Georgian government and teaching of the Armenian language. Georgia has failed to sign and ratify the Council of Europe's European Charter for Regional or Minority Languages.

Azerbaijan complicates Georgia-Armenia relations. Azerbaijan is used by Georgia as an alternative energy supplier to Russia. Azerbaijani investments in the gas distribution system of Georgia and the sale of oil and gas are tied to conditions of limiting access for Armenia.

For example, Azerbaijan has influenced the routes of key corridors such as the Baku-Tbilisi-Ceyhan oil pipeline and the Baku-Tbilisi-Kars railroad construction, both bypassing Armenia.

Georgia offers Armenia its only land connection with Europe and access to its Black Sea ports, and most Armenian trade with Turkey currently goes through Georgia.

Armenia does have the advantage of having an influential diaspora community in Georgia. This community cannot be viewed as homogenous; differences exist between many Armenians integrated in Georgia and those that reside in Javakheti, who continue to uphold and value Armenian traditions. There are also Armenian communities in Abkhazia and South Ossetia.

Consideration should be given how to promote closer relations in new and different ways. Armenians in Georgia's capital, Tbilisi, constituted 40 percent of its population early in the 19th century. Many significant cultural Armenian icons were from Tbilisi, such as composer Sayat-Nova; internationally acclaimed composer Aram Khachaturian; world chess champion Tigran Petrossian; and many others. This monumental legacy that Armenia-Georgia share should be celebrated as a historic link. An opportunity to strengthen tourism around this legacy.

In June 2024, Armenia supported Georgia by voting in favour of a UN resolution calling for the right to return of Georgians to Abkhazia and South Ossetia. The Armenian vote was referred in some circles as a 'historic moment.'[51]

There are many opportunities to consider, and one in particular that the Armenian government needs to address is the trade imbalance. Georgia consistently runs a positive trade balance with Armenia, exporting more to Armenia than it imports. This is partly driven by Armenia's reliance on Georgian ports on the Black Sea, and a logistics corridor to Russia. If the goal is to grow exports to Georgia, Armenia can focus on value added goods, complementary services, and seasonal supply advantages.

Finally, another area for consideration is the introduction of multilateral visa schemes with Georgia (similar to the Schengen model) to promote multi-country tours in the Caucasus. Both governments should work with tourism operators to help with the influx to both countries.

European Union: Cautious Embrace

Armenia's relations with the European Union (EU) has to be balanced with Russia. The arc of Armenia–EU relations has not been linear. In 1999, Armenia joined the Partnership and Cooperation Agreement (PCA), a framework that laid the groundwork for political and economic dialogue. This was followed by the European Neighbourhood Policy and later the Eastern Partnership in 2009.

In 2013, a pivot took place when Armenia opted to join the Russian-led Eurasian Economic Union (EEU), which momentarily threatened to derail deeper EU integration. But in a moment of pragmatic diplomacy, the Comprehensive and Enhanced Partnership Agreement (CEPA) was born in 2017. CEPA was not just a second-best option, it was a uniquely tailored arrangement that allowed Armenia to deepen ties with the EU without compromising its other geopolitical commitments.

CEPA represents an ambitious roadmap, with more than 350 articles covering judicial reform, environmental protection, trade standards, public administration, and digital governance. It is an institutional scaffolding for transformation.

Then the Artsakh war in 2023 reset some previous allegiances and led to a deeper distrust of Russia within Armenia.

In March 2025, Armenia passed a law initiating the process for eventual EU membership. These moves have led to tensions with Russia, as officials have warned that pursuing EU membership is incompatible with continued participation in the EEU.

Furthermore, the EU has been providing monitors along the Armenian-Azerbaijani border. Following Azerbaijani protests, the Armenian government agreed to withdraw European Union monitors from the Armenian-Azerbaijani border, if a peace deal is settled.[52] The EU has a monitoring mission in Armenia along the border of Azerbaijan to monitor any violations of the ceasefire, and its mandate was extended until February 2027.

While the monitoring mission lacks enforcement powers, it has effectively patrolled border areas, monitoring ceasefire violations, and providing credible reporting that counters Azerbaijani disinformation campaigns.

As observed by Sossi Tatikyan, a former official at the Armenian Foreign Ministry, the mission's visible presence has served as a soft deterrent against escalations. Significantly, the only major post-deployment escalation occurred in March 2024, in the village of Nerkin Hand, an area then under Russian oversight rather than the EU monitoring mission – highlighting the mission's stabilising influence. The mission has helped keep international attention focused on the Armenia–Azerbaijan border, reinforcing the EU's broader geopolitical engagement.[53]

The EU has been a significant source of aid to the Armenian Government, the largest provider of financial support and a reform partner in Armenia. It is estimated Armenia received around €185 million under the EU's Neighbourhood Policy between 2017 and 2020.[54]

In 2021, EU Commissioner for Neighbourhood and Enlargement Oliver Varhelyi announced that the EU will be granting approximately $3.1 billion in aid to Armenia, a 62 percent increase than the amount promised before.[55]

In April 2024, the EU announced a €270 million Resilience and Growth Plan for Armenia for 2024-2027, which includes €200 million in grant assistance and €70 million in grant funding for Armenia.[56]

A year later, in April 2025, it was announced that the visa liberalisation process is actively proceeding and that Armenia would introduce biometric passports by 2026, a step towards potential visa-free travel to the EU.

EU member states combined have a greater bilateral trade with Armenia than the combined EEU States including Russia. In 2023, Armenia's bilateral trade with the EU topped $2.7 billion, making the EU one of Armenia's biggest and most important economic partners.[57] However, this also needs to be balanced against security. Armenia is outside the NATO framework which most EU states enjoy, and Armenia finds itself at a delicate nexus where the EU cannot provide security assurances, despite efforts by some individual members like France which provide military equipment.

That said, in July 2024, the EU approved the allocation of €10 million to the Armenia's Armed Forces. This marked the first ever funding assistance of this kind. The funding will be used to increase the material and technical capabilities of Armenia's army.

In February 2023, in an opinion survey, 60 percent of Armenians said they trusted the EU more than any other international institution, and 74 percent thought relations between the EU and Armenia were good.[58]

In January 2025, an opinion survey conducted by MPG found that a majority of Armenians believed Armenia would join the EU in the following ten years. In addition, 55 percent of participants had a positive opinion when asked how they felt about the draft law on EU accession.[59]

Although Armenia has reduced its security dependence on Russia and the CSTO, it remains structurally tied to the Eurasian Economic Union (EEU) through trade, labour migration, and energy. This dependency limits Armenia's ability to fully align with EU economic standards. This deep entanglement needs to be untangled to reduce dependency.

In the harsh reality of no allies, economic integration to an organisation like the EU needs to be decoupled from security and energy constraints.

Many countries in the world have to balance strong economic relations with China, with security dependency or alignment with the United States. Armenia faces a similar scenario between the EU and Russia and must navigate with precision with a 360 foreign policy approach.

Azerbaijan – Peace at What Price?

Armenia and Azerbaijan had formal relations between 1918 and 1921, during their brief independence prior to their Sovietisation.

Upon the establishment of the USSR in 1922, the Azerbaijan Soviet Socialist Republic (SSR) and the Armenian SSR were initially part of the Transcaucasian SFSR and became separate entities within the union in 1936.

One lasting impact on their relations was the decision Joseph Stalin, the People's Commissar for Nationalities, made in 1921 determining Nagorno-Karabagh's political status. In July that year, the Caucasus Bureau of the Communist Party debated whether Nagorno-Karabagh should be part of the Armenian SSR or the Azerbaijan SSR. They initially decided Nagorno-Karabagh should be included in Armenia, before the decision was reversed under Stalin's influence. This led to the formal establishment of the Nagorno-Karabagh Autonomous Oblast (NKAO) within Azerbaijan in 1923.

In 1988, under the influence of glasnost and perestroika movements seeking greater freedoms in the Soviet Union, mass rallies began in Nagorno-Karabagh's capital Stepanakert, as well as Yerevan, demanding that Nagorno-Karabagh be united with the Armenian SSR. In February 1988, the autonomous oblast voted to be transferred from Azerbaijan to Armenia, which was rejected by Moscow and Baku.

Pogroms followed, targeting Armenians in Azerbaijan, and then, following the collapse of the Soviet Union, both States started fighting, which concluded in a peace deal in 1994, where Armenians controlled the territory.

It is worth noting that prior to 1988, around 500,000 Armenians lived in Azerbaijan and an estimated 170,000 Azeris in Armenia. Those communities no longer exist today.

There remains distrust between both States. Azerbaijan provocatively labels Armenia as 'West Azerbaijan', they hold Armenian political prisoners in custody offering no fair trial following the Nagorno-Karabagh conflict, and consistently make demands such as a transport route through the Zangezur corridor, the southernmost point in Armenia. Furthermore, there are numerous border villages which have been claimed by Azerbaijan within its territory.

After many months of negotiation, the joint declaration for peace was signed by Armenia and Azerbaijan at the White House on 8 August 2025. The declaration was signed following concessions from Armenia, including removing territorial claims referencing Nagorno-Karabagh from its constitution's preamble; Armenia committed to the non-deployment of third-party forces on the shared

Figure 1. Azerbaijan's territorial occupation of
Republic of Armenia sovereign territory
gained during the Artsakh conflict.

Source: Ruben Melkonyan, Varuzhan Geghamyan, *The Armenian Wedge of the Path of Turan, The Issue of 'Zangezur Corridor'*, [n.i.], 2025.

border; and both sides agreeing to withdraw legal claims currently filed in international courts against each other.

There remain many obstacles to achieving peace. Concessions to achieve peace is not reciprocal, meaning there has been too much weight placed on Azerbaijani claims and demands. Finally, there is no guarantee peace will hold. Azerbaijan with the upper military hand has constantly been provocative.

In 2023, President of Azerbaijan, Ilham Aliyev was stating that Armenians in Karabagh could stay if they took Azerbaijani citizenship,[60] at the same time satellite imagery showed what appeared to be 'concentration camp,'[61] buildings to detain Armenians who may have fought in the war. President Aliyev claims he only has issues with 'criminal separatists', but who is a criminal separatist? A soldier defending their ancestral land, the widow who actively helped and supported her soldier husband, an Artsakh government official attending the needs of the local population, or is it the Armenian business person who invested in the region and created jobs, or a tourist who visited the land, but did so without approval from Azerbaijan? In this scenario, everyone could potentially be labelled a 'criminal separatist'.

The Armenian government, which is tired of war and conflict at this moment, may not have the appetite to demand autonomy for Artsakh at this stage. The joint declaration for peace seeks to nullify legitimate disputes which have not justly been resolved.

Neighbouring countries across the globe often have disputes, but this doesn't mean that they cannot have relations. A declaration of peace in its current form doesn't resolve underlying concerns. Nor is it a peace treaty – if anything, it just signals intent. The focus should be on establishing relations without preconditions.

In an ideal world everyone wants peace – but at what price? Time will tell if the joint declaration for peace serves Armenia's legitimate interests. The details of this declaration and negotiating tactics surrounding it, will be examined further in Chapter Nine – The Art of the Deal.

S20: Opportunity to Lead

The notion of an organisation called the S20 is a concept introduced by former President of Armenia, Armen Sarkissian.[62] That is an organisation which represents the interests of small states at global forums.

Other similar organisations include the G20, or Group of Twenty, which is an international forum consisting of the globe's largest 19 economies and the European Union. It was established in 1999 to bring together these economies to discuss and coordinate policy on global economic issues, particularly those related to financial stability. The G7 or Group of Seven, is an informal forum of seven of the world's largest advanced economies. The G7 focuses on issues such as economic policy, international trade, security, and global governance.

Small states are generally characterised by their small population, geographic size, or economic capacity. The specific classification can vary depending on the context or criteria.

For the purpose of this exercise, small states could be populations with less than ten million, and have limited natural resources, thereby having to leverage disproportionately innovation and enterprise. Within this framework, the S20 members can effectively learn from one another, and collectively be a force, or represent the interest of their States at global forums.

As Sarkissian recounts in his concept of the S20, *"the defining characteristic of the Small States Club is not their geographical extent or population, but the prosperity and achievements these states have realised ... Their shared story revolves around success in various spheres – from technological innovation and economic performance to social development."*[63]

In the World Intellectual Property Organisation Global Innovation Index,[64] six of the top ten countries would be considered small states, (if we make an exception by including Sweden which has a population slightly above ten million). These countries are Singapore, Switzerland, Sweden, Denmark, Finland, and The Netherlands. The Bloomberg Global Innovation Index[65] lists eight of the top ten being small states, including those listed and Israel and Austria.

Although Armenia is not listed on these Indexes, it does rank strongly in another category which would be considered smart – that being IQ, short for intelligent quotient. The International IQ registry[66] found Armenia ranked 9th globally.

Armenia could proactively take the initiative and advocate for the formation of the S20 and follow operational models like the G20.

In the G20, the country holding the presidency is responsible for organising and hosting the meetings for that year, setting the agenda, and providing administrative support. The host country's government typically assigns specific officials to act as the secretariat for that year. They coordinate with other member states, international organisations, and stakeholders to prepare for and manage activities during their presidency.

It has been proven in the past that you do not need to be a superpower to be the lead instigator in the formation of a global forum. The Asia-Pacific Economic Cooperation (APEC), which was established in 1989 as an initiative to foster economic growth, cooperation, trade, and investment in the Asia-Pacific region, has 21 member economies, representing a significant portion of global GDP and trade.

Its formation was driven by the recognition of increasing interdependence among economies in the region and the need for a collaborative platform to address shared challenges and opportunities. Bob Hawke, the Australian Prime Minister at the time, proposed the idea of APEC during a speech in Seoul, South Korea, in January 1989. He emphasised the need for regional economic cooperation and dialogue to sustain economic growth. This proposal was part of Australia's broader strategy to engage more deeply with Asia-Pacific economies.

Similarly, the need for cooperation among small states, particularly smart small states, should be part of Armenia's strategy to engage more deeply with similarly sized economies that have similar challenges.

Some of the criticisms of such organisations is that they are unable to enforce agreements between member states. Agreements could be very broad, rendering them to be meaningless.

However, if an organisation like the S20 could be formed as a collective, it could represent some of the most innovative countries in the globe, providing a platform to engage larger states that are represented in the G7 or G20, and be a vehicle to help drive trade, innovation and leveraging best practices. It could place Armenia in a unique position to engage as well as broaden its influence globally.

Soft Power

As outlined in the first edition of Smart Nation, Armenia has at its disposal many resources to project soft power, particularly through its well connected diaspora, and highly tech savvy Armenian youth.

Soft power is a concept that describes the ability to attract and co-opt rather than coerce, such as hard power, which typically uses force or finance as a means of persuasion.

Soft power is the ability to shape the preferences of others through appeal and attraction. A defining feature of soft power is that it is non-coercive; the currency of soft power is culture, political values, and foreign policies. Credibility is a valuable resource.

Soft power is often displayed by Armenians in the diaspora who are in prominent positions in business, media, and entertainment. Just one example is that of Patrick Ben David of Armenian and Assyrian descent who hosts one of the most popular podcasts in the United States called PBD podcast which has around three million subscribers. Such is his influence that guests to his program is a rollcall of global celebrities, personalities, and political leaders, including President Trump. In one episode, while interviewing Prime Minister of Israel Benjamin Netanyahu, he was able to have the Prime Minister acknowledge the Armenian, Assyrian and Greek genocides, something which had not been publicly acknowledged before.[67]

According to the 2025 Soft Power World Rankings Index, the United States is on top, followed by China, UK, Japan, Germany, France, Canada, Switzerland, Italy, and United Arab Emirates.[68] Armenia is ranked 93rd out of 193 member states, and improved its ranking of 106th in the previous year.

One of the most recognisable soft power plays is China's 'panda diplomacy', a classic and highly symbolic form of soft power, in which the Chinese government loans giant pandas to foreign zoos as gestures of friendship, goodwill, or strategic partnership. This approach dates back decades and serves multiple diplomatic, cultural, and geopolitical purposes

Other than Switzerland and UAE, who are small nation states ranked in the top ten, other small states that perform well include Denmark (18th), Belgium (19th), Singapore (21st), Qatar (22nd), Finland (21st), and New Zealand (25th).

Taking a comparison of Armenia versus neighbouring states – Turkey is 26th, Georgia 59th, Iran 62nd, Azerbaijan 81st.

This Index measures soft power across eight pillars and 35 nation brand attributes. The eight pillars include business and trade, international relations, education and science, culture and heritage, governance, media and communications, sustainable future, and people and values.

Armenia's low ranking in the Global Soft Power Index is not due to a single factor but rather a combination of visibility, influence, and resource limitations. Soft power is largely a perception game. Armenia lacks strong brand visibility globally, especially outside its diaspora. According to Brand Finance's methodology, countries with low recognition tend to score poorly across all categories, regardless of internal progress.

Armenia rarely sets the global news agenda. It is more often portrayed as a victim of conflict or crisis (eg, Nagorno-Karabagh conflict 2023) than as a proactive global actor. Unlike Israel, South Korea, or even UAE, Armenia does not have major international broadcasters, global cultural products, or viral public diplomacy campaigns.

Armenia is often seen through the lens of its geopolitical fragility—a small landlocked country caught between Russia, Turkey, and Iran. This can damage perceptions of governance, influence, and stability, key pillars in the index.

Armenia lacks a coordinated branding strategy, a cultural diplomacy agency, or a soft power task force in this regard, which it should consider establishing

In the first edition of Smart Nation it was highlighted of Armenia's then tourism campaign titled 'Noah's Route: Your Route' with picturesque videos promoting Armenia as a tourist destination, which was widely circulated by diaspora communities.

The economy's small size limits Armenia's ability to invest in international aid, infrastructure, global media, and innovation ecosystems—all critical to soft power. While there is tech success stories, there is insufficient global promotion of these success stories.

Armenia's diaspora is one of its greatest soft power assets—but it is not strategically mobilised. Unlike Israel or Greece, Armenia has no formal program to integrate diaspora into public diplomacy or soft power initiatives at scale.

There are a number of things Armenia can do to improve its image: it requires a more effective and impactful external and global communications plan. To project soft power requires a sophisticated external communications plan, utilising real global expertise, non-political agenda, and projecting the nation's assets.

As mentioned earlier in the book, Armenia could seek to host significant events like the Global AI Summit, and leveraging national assets like the Armenian National Philharmonic Orchestra (ANPO) for overseas performances. The orchestra can play a vital role in strengthening ties between nations that Armenia intends to pursue closer relations with. It is also an important way of disarming preconceived views on Armenia. A striking example was when the orchestra performed at Iran's historic Persepolis archaeological complex,[69] on the occasion of its 100th anniversary, but also a symbolism of ties between two civilisations dating back more than 2,500 years.

An overly ambitious goal could be establishing a global Armenian Media News Channel. Many countries have one example France 24 (France); Deutsche Welle (Germany); Al Jazeera (Qatar); Russia Today; TRT World (Turkey); Channel News Asia (Singapore).

Given Armenia is a member of the International Organisation of La Francophonie (OIF) — also known simply as the Francophonie, it could consider some type of media partnership with France 24, which would broaden its broadcast reach.

Armenia became a full member of the OIF in 2012, after previously holding observer and associate member status. In a demonstration of 'soft power, Yerevan hosted the 17th Francophonie Summit in October 2018, bringing together leaders from more than 80 French-speaking nations, with the event attracting significant media attention, as well as among the participating countries.

Another perceived attempt was when Armenian Prime Minister Pashinyan participated in an interview with Turkish media (ten outlets) in Yerevan on March 13, 2025, where he spoke about normalisation, border reopening, genocide recognition priorities, and peace talks—with all exchanges in Armenian. However, this was somewhat ill fated when it was realised this exchange with Turkish journalists had been invited to Yerevan at the Armenian government's expense.[70]

A major win has been Armenia's selection to host COP17. This is the 17th meeting of the UN Convention on Biological Diversity, taking place in Yerevan in October 2026. Armenia's significant strides in biodiversity conservation and its commitment to sustainable development helped secure the bid. Armenia has prioritised biodiversity, implementing legislative and institutional reforms, protecting endangered species, and effectively managing protected areas, according to the selection committee.

Neighbouring Azerbaijan has been more effective in its efforts to project soft power. Flushed with oil money, it has targeted many international events putting the country on the global map, despite its atrocious human rights record. The most notable have been hosting COP29 in November 2024 in Baku, the most significant climate summit in the globe (which required the support of Armenia, and was provided as part of a deal involving the release of Armenian prisoners held in Azerbaijan). COP29 helped disguise Azerbaijan's export of oil which, ironically, has contributed to the climate crisis. The Summit hosts used the event to showcase its sustainable energy credentials, while illegally detaining Armenian political prisoners at the same time.

In 2017, Baku hosted the F1 Grand Prix, taking over what was previously known as the European Grand Prix. An annual fixture which draws a global audience and major global sponsors attracting worldwide attention.

In 2025, Azerbaijan and Uzbekistan officially submitted a joint bid to host the 2027 FIFA U20 World Cup, marking their interest in hosting a FIFA youth tournament for the first time.

Azerbaijan has also attracted international artists to play concerts, including Justin Timberlake, Shakira, Rihanna, and Christina Aguilera. In August 2025, the Armenian government contributed $6 million towards Jennifer Lopez's concert in Armenia in August 2025, attracting an estimated 15,000 international visitors, and reportedly injecting $13.3 million into the economy.[71]

It's worth noting Azerbaijan won the Eurovision Song Contest in 2011, which gave it hosting rights the following year. Armenia has a history of performing well in the contest, often making it to the finals, but it has not won the competition yet.

Rather than assertively projecting soft power, Armenia is often a target of soft power. The EU is a case in point with its provision of technical assistance and tied to reform conditionality to Armenia; Turkish television shows are widely viewed in Armenia, subtly exporting values, lifestyle, and gender dynamics of modern Turkey; Russia uses media (Sputnik Armenia) and Russia Today as well as church diplomacy (Armenian Apostolic Church ties with the Moscow Patriarchate) to assert moral and civilizational affinity; France actively promotes cultural ties and symbolic gestures such as President Macron's public speeches highlighting shared history and values and commemorating landmark events such as the Armenian genocide anniversaries.

Macron has also occasionally tweeted in Armenian, for example commemorating the death of legendary French Armenian singer Charles Aznavour in October 2018, by tweeting "He, who knew the tragedy of history, gave a voice to those who had been silenced," "Հիմնվին Թրանսիացի և խորապես կապված իր Հայ արմատներին..."

Armenia's projection of soft power is neither soft nor powerful. It is uncoordinated and lacks vision, and needs a vital boost. The government should consider establishing a taskforce to deal with the issue.

Chapter Three

Women and Wellbeing

Women's Rights

The Armenian republic of 1918–20 was one of the first nations in the world to give women the right to vote, and eight percent of the elected members of its parliament were women. The first female ambassador in the world was Dr. Diana Abgar (Abgaryan), Ambassador of Armenia in Japan during Armenia's first republic.

Mother Armenia, a large statue symbolising the female personification of Armenia, stands majestically overlooking the city of Yerevan. The Mother Armenia statue symbolises peace through strength and is reminiscent of some of the prominent female figures in Armenian history.

However, domestic violence and the mistreatment of women in Armenia is a serious problem. It is a national shame, underreported, and unseen.

Since the last publishing of this book, matters have become worse. In 2024, authorities recorded 1,360 cases of domestic and family violence, marking a nearly threefold increase from the 508 cases reported in 2023.[72] Tragically, 13 murders were linked to domestic violence in 2024, up from three cases in 2023.[73]

There are numerous reasons why domestic violence takes place, including cultural stereotyping and attitudes towards women; significant psychological scars of warfare which are yet to be fully understood; as well as stress, whether it be economic or otherwise.

Armenia has implemented some amendments to its domestic violence legislation. These include: expanded definitions whereby the law now encompasses various forms of abuse, such as forced medical interventions, hindering access to healthcare, and controlling behaviours; criminalisation of stalking, which has been established as a standalone criminal offense; protective measures, including amendments setting minimum times for urgent intervention measures, and extended periods for protective orders, thus facilitating more effective responses to threats; and support for survivors to have priority access to free healthcare services, as well as shelters mandated to be accessible to individuals with disabilities.

Armenia has also introduced its first unified digital system for recording domestic violence cases.[74] This joint initiative between the United Nations Population Fund (UNFPA) and Armenia's Ministry of Labour and Social Affairs contain comprehensive information on each reported incident, including a log of all proceedings and services provided to the survivor.

There remain a number of additional measures that should be taken such as: mandatory gender-sensitive training for police and judiciary; creating specialised domestic violence units within police departments; and ensuring protective orders are issued quickly and consistently enforced.

In Yerevan, there is reportedly only two shelters dedicated for survivors of domestic violence abuse.[75] The limited availability of shelter spaces often leads survivors to remain in abusive situations due to a lack of safe alternatives. Expanding shelter capacity and support services is essential, particularly in regional centres of Armenia, to provide survivors with safe environments and comprehensive assistance, including legal aid, psychological counselling, and rehabilitation programs. Enhancing these services is a crucial step toward effectively combating domestic violence in Armenia.

Another step the Armenian government should consider is appointing Ambassadors to lead a national education awareness campaign to prevent domestic violence. These could include prominent males, which the male population looks up to.

In the last edition of Smart Nation, according to the Global Gender Gap Report for 2013, Armenia ranked 94th out of 136 countries for gender equality.[65] In the Global Gender Report for 2024, Armenia ranks 64th out of 146 countries.[76] The index evaluates countries by four key criteria, including economic participation and opportunity; educational attainment; health and survival; and political empowerment.

One way to address this matter is to have a dedicated Minister for Women, which is something that was proposed in the first edition of

Smart Nation. The Armenian Government should consider appointing a minister for women, to be responsible not only for the protection of women from domestic abuse and trafficking, but also to foster and encourage women into leadership positions.

In Armenia, the Council on Women's Affairs, established in 2019 and chaired by the Deputy Prime Minister, serves as a national mechanism to ensure equal rights and opportunities for women and men, assisting in their involvement in democratic processes. This Council could be remodelled under the Ministry for Women.

Empowering women not only helps with diversity but would help the economy. It should be noted that Armenia's female population is estimated at around 54 percent.[77] According to the Peterson Institute for International Economics, a study of 22,000 publicly traded companies across 91 countries found that having women in the highest corporate offices is correlated with increased profitability.[70]

At present, issues related to women's rights and gender equality are primarily managed by the Ministry of Labor and Social Affairs. However, there needs to be a dedicated emphasis on the issue of women's rights in Armenia.

Other models to consider are countries that already have such a Ministry. Many nations have a dedicated Ministry such as Australia, New Zealand, France, South Korea, Brazil and many others.

There is much the Armenian government can and should do in this regard, and a dedicated Ministry would not only would strengthen the government's commitment to achieve gender equality as a national priority, but also enable it to undertake a whole-of-government approach.

Happiness and Morale

In the previous edition of Smart Nation, it mentioned that Armenia ranked 121st out of 157 countries in the World Happiness report of 2016.[71] A poor result by many standards.[72] The World Happiness report of 2025 has shown a marked improvement, with Armenia moving to 87th place out of 147 countries.[78] This compares to its neighbours Azerbaijan ranking 106th and Georgia 91st.

The report measures a wide variety of areas including based on six key indices covering GDP per capita; social support; healthy life expectancy; freedom to make life choices; generosity; and perceptions of corruption. Why has Armenia improved?

There are a range of reasons including economic growth, social resilience, and institutional progress. Armenia's GDP per capita has been steadily increasing, especially post-2016 and despite international turbulence, its economy has remained resilient. Although corruption has not been eliminated, the perceptions of corruption have declined since a decade ago, resulting in another contributing factor.

An area which Armenia may take things for granted is safety. In the World Happiness report of 2025, Armenia was ranked 29th out of 147 countries in the following safety measure: having your wallet to be returned by a stranger. According to the Numbeo Safety Index 2025,[79] Yerevan is ranked the 21st safest city in the world compared to around 400 other cities, a remarkable score. When compared toother countries, Armenia is ranked as the 8th safest country in the world!

This is a comparative advantage for Armenia, which is not always fully leveraged. Safety is a major contributor to happiness and morale, both at the individual and societal levels. While the World Happiness Index doesn't label 'safety' as a standalone category, it's deeply embedded in several of the key factors used in the rankings.

The World Happiness report is important because there is a direct correlation between happiness (and morale) to the nation's productivity, which has a direct bearing on its economy. In the workplace, happy employees can contribute to higher productivity, sales, and creativity. A study in the *Harvard Business Review* found that happy employees demonstrated on average 31 percent higher productivity, 37 percent higher sales, with creativity three times higher.[73] How does this apply to nations? Think of the citizen as the employee – or as many governments may now refer to them, when they use their services, customers. And consider the government as the employer.

The report found that inequality was strongly associated with unhappiness, a stark finding for rich countries like the United States, where rising disparities in income, wealth, health, and wellbeing have fuelled political discontent.

The previous edition of Smart Nation sought Armenia to have a plan to be ranked in the top 50 by 2020, and aim to be in the top 20 in the decade thereafter. Although there is positive movement, this indicates there is more work to be done. This book is revising these figures to top 50 by 2030, and be in top 20 by 2050.

An improved result will demonstrate Armenia has made strides toward equality and improved many of its governance structures, which will result in increased productivity and a reflection of improved living standards.

Creating a Sense of Urgency

In the last edition of Smart Nation it was observed that there was a general sense of a lack of urgency in Armenia. *"For those who travel to Armenia, particularly from western nations, one thing becomes apparent very quickly: there appears to be a lack of urgency. This attitude is displayed in various forms. It is most apparent in late-morning starts to work and lax customer service, and occasionally comes across as general apathy. Walking the streets of major global cities, people appear rushed; they walk with a sense of purpose and urgency. For some, Armenia's mindset may appear a refreshing one. Not having to worry about small things, there may be some sense to this thinking. However, many successful people, be it in sport, business, or otherwise, set themselves apart by creating a sense of urgency. Without urgency, mediocrity and complacency prevails, which leads to failure. Urgency needs to be ignited and then maintained."*

Although a lack of urgency prevails in some areas, a number of factors has created more urgency. A noticeable impact is traffic congestion in Yerevan, which has been driven by a rise in vehicle numbers. For a population of just over one million people, Yerevan has more than half a million privately registered vehicles,[80] a city originally designed for a much smaller population.

The negatives is increased air and noise pollution, however conversely this can create an increased sense of urgency. Another noticeable change is people starting work earlier. More than fifteen years ago, you could only find a handful of venues that served breakfast – nowadays there are many venues that offer this service reflective of a bustling active city.

A number of steps are required to create a sense of urgency, as conveyed by John Kotter, author of a *Sense of Urgency*.[74] First, bring the outside in. A view that 'we know best' reduces urgency. Second, behave with urgency every day. Third, find opportunity in crises. People often view a crisis as a time to limit damage control but, in fact, it is an opportunity. Fourth, counter the view that the current situation is fine.

Time is limited. People must make the best use of it. Armenia, the Smart Nation, cannot be left behind.

Chapter Four

The Modern Fortress

The history of the Armenian nation is woven through various kingdoms over thousands of years. From the Urartian, Artaxiad dynasty, and Bagratid — all of which made extensive and strategic use of fortresses as core elements of national defence. These fortifications were not just military installations, they were symbols of sovereignty, centres of administration, and critical to the survival of Armenian kingdoms across millennia of conflict.

Fortresses were built in massive stone on mountain tops and ridges to dominate trade routes and river valleys. They were strongholds for military defence, administrative centres overseeing provinces, and safeguards for irrigation systems, and armouries, then critical infrastructure.

In the ancient city of Ani, which borders current day Turkey and Armenia, its fortress and walls were legendary — thick, multi-layered defences with towers, moats, and iron gates.

In ancient times, fortresses made use of the landscape, especially mountainous ones, ideal for elevated positions. They could withstand prolonged sieges, invasions were slowed or repelled by defenders using narrow passes, fortified gorges, and layered walls. They combined geographical advantage, engineering, and resilience into structures that protected the heart of the nation across centuries of foreign threat.

Those times have passed and in the modern era Armenia needs a reinvigorated defence posture that will continue to enable its survival for another millennia.

Armenia's Iron Dome

Armenia needs its own Iron Dome. Fortresses were Armenia's Iron Dome of antiquity.

The Iron Dome refers to Israel's air defence system designed to intercept and destroy short-range rockets, artillery shells, and mortars that threaten civilian populations and infrastructure.

It is a highly effective and successful system. It is designed to intercept and destroy short-range rockets, artillery shells, and mortars fired from distances of four to seventy kilometres, especially those targeting civilian areas. It is claimed that interception rates are more than 90 percent for rockets.

In addition to the Iron Dome, Israel also employs other defence layers including: David's Sling, designed for medium- to long-range threats; Arrow system, for long-range ballistic missiles; and Iron Beam, a laser-based system for close-range threats. These layers form what is referred to as Israel's multi-tiered missile defence system.

In Israel's conflict with Iran in 2025, more than 370 missiles and hundreds of drones targeted sites in Israel, with an overall interception rate of 80-90 percent by Israel's multilayered defence systems.[81]

National security and Armenia's defence posture are critical for national survival. In public polls, the Armenian public has rated national security and border issues as Armenia's most important concerns, upwards of 40 percent.[82]

Armenia's military is estimated to comprise 45,000 active-duty personnel, and the country maintains a reserve force estimated at around 210,000 individuals who have served in the past 15 years. In comparison with neighbouring Azerbaijan, its military is reported to have more than 65,000 active-duty personnel, along with 300,000 reservists and 15,000 paramilitary members.

In 2024, the Armenian government announced a 20 percent increase in military spending, allocating around ₹665 billion to the Ministry of Defence.[83] This marks a substantial rise from previous years. In 2023, military expenditure was around $1.28 billion, reflecting a 46 percent increase from 2022. Despite these increases, Armenia's defence budget remains lower than Azerbaijan. In 2025,

Azerbaijan's military spending was projected to reach around $5.5 billion, maintaining a significant advantage over Armenia.[84]

Then, in August 2025, after the signing of the declaration of peace between Armenia and Azerbaijan, Prime Minister Pashinyan indicated the country's defence spending may not see an increase in 2026, saying it was 'logical.'[85] In September 2025, the draft state budget approved by the government showed a 15 percent decrease in military spending for 2026. If this were to occur, it would be extremely naïve and place Armenia at increased vulnerability.

Armenia's air defence relies on Soviet and Russian made systems, including long-range surface-to-air missile system, medium and short-range air defence systems, and modern short range system capable of intercepting precision guided munitions, drones, and aircraft. It also has capabilities for low-altitude threats, and electronic warfare systems.

Compared to the Iron Dome, Armenia lacks high volume short-range rocket and artillery interception, rapid response with automated radar-guided targeting, and urban area protection. It also lacks an effective interceptor system for incoming rockets or drone swarms. Nor does it have an integrated, layered air defence network that autonomously classifies and prioritises threats like Iron Dome.

During the Artsakh conflict of 2020, Azerbaijan with the help of Turkey neutralised Armenia's air defences early in the conflict, leaving Armenian forces exposed. They deployed electronic warfare systems to jam and spoof Armenian radars, and their real-time intelligence and satellite surveillances coordinated through Turkish advisors were able to identify and destroy high-value targets, ensuring their military superiority.

The collapse of Armenia's air defence in the 2020 Artsakh war was not just a failure, it was a technological shock for the country known for its technological prowess in the region. Soviet era systems were outmatched by modern, integrated drone warfare.

Although steps are underway to modernise defences, it needs to be driven by significant urgency. Some of this includes diversifying sources for military equipment, moving beyond a reliance on Russia, and strengthening military ties with France, India, Greece and the EU for defence procurement and training.

The harsh reality is that this exposed vulnerability requires an urgent need to build local capabilities and using Armenia's technological capabilities invested in its defence. Given this urgency, the Government should consider providing incentives for technology companies that build capabilities that directly benefit Armenia's defence.

As most eloquently conveyed by Armenia's most beloved poets Payruyr Sevak, "*Մենք ենք մեր փրկիչները*" which translates to "We are our own saviours."

Porcupine Defence Plan

The Iron Dome and other defence initiatives need to be part of a well developed porcupine defence strategy.

A porcupine defence strategy or plan is a metaphor used to describe a defensive posture where a country or entity makes itself so well-defended and resilient that any attack becomes excessively costly and unattractive for an aggressor, much like trying to attack a porcupine with its sharp quills.

Several countries, some of them small with hostile neighbours often apply this plan, including Israel, Finland, Switzerland, Singapore, and the Baltic states of Lithuania, Latvia and Estonia.

What they have in common is cost effective methods to offset adversary advantages, prepared citizenry, civilians trained or prepared for wartime contingencies, geographic or structural fortifications, exploiting natural terrain or building defensive infrastructure, and strategic alliances, partnerships with larger powers or alliances to deter aggression.

A notable example is Taiwan, which is under constant threat from China. China which asserts a one-China policy, claims Taiwan as its territory, or as it refers to it, as Chinese Taipai. Taiwan's military strategy has undergone a fundamental transformation. Instead of trying to match China's military capabilities head-to-head, Taiwan is focusing on a defence doctrine that emphasises mobility and cost-effectiveness. This involves deploying mobile missiles, sea mines, and drone swarms that could inflict significant damage on any invading force. The goal is not to win a conventional war but to create a situation where the costs of invasion outweigh the benefits.

The advent of a modern military means conflicts can be influenced by relatively inexpensive drones and portable missiles to counter expensive military forces. The aim of a porcupine defence plan is to inflict maximum pain on an invading force rather than seeking traditional battlefield dominance. For example, a Chinese Type 055 destroyer costs around $890 million, while Taiwan's Hsiung Feng III anti-ship missiles cost approximately $3.5 million each. If Taiwan were to launch three missiles to sink one destroyer, it would achieve an 85:1 exchange ratio in its favour.[86]

Finland, with a population of just over 5.5 million, employs a 'total defence' doctrine, where not just the military, but society at large, government, civil institutions, infrastructure, and civilians, are integrated into defence planning, targeted against Russia. Finland has vast forests, lakes, and harsh winters, terrain that favours defenders and makes large scale armoured offensives costly. Defence plans are built around using geography to delay and bleed an aggressor. Finland invests heavily in long-range precision strike weapons that can hold aggressors and supply lines at risk. Finland has one of the world's most extensive civilian shelter networks, capable of housing most of its urban population in case of attack. Although it recently joined NATO, Finland's strategy still assumes it must be able to resist alone initially.

For Armenia, a porcupine defence plan is not only required, but is urgent for vulnerable border points it has with Azerbaijan, and especially for its southern Syunik province, where Azerbaijan has constantly threatened to invade.

Intelligence

The history and importance of national intelligence organisations span centuries, evolving from ancient court spies into sophisticated modern agencies that shape global politics, security, and power. These organisations play a critical role in national defence, foreign policy, and internal stability. In the modern era, national intelligence organisations evoke images of espionage and spies, but they are important in detecting and neutralising external and internal threats, from terrorist plots to foreign invasions to cyberattacks.

They have a multitude of other functions, including providing heads of state with insights into adversaries' intentions, aiding in diplomacy or military decision making, tracking extremist networks and coordinating with police forces to prevent attacks, defend critical infrastructure and conduct offensive cyber operations against adversaries, monitor global financial flows, trade negotiations, and technological espionage, both defending against and conducting information warfare — as seen in election interference.

The most notable of these organisations globally is the United States' Central Intelligence Agency (CIA). Small states like Israel have robust intelligence capabilities, such as Mossad and Shin Bet, which are renowned for their ability to pre-empt threats and conduct counterterrorism operations. Furthermore, Israel is a leader in cybersecurity and uses offensive and defensive cyber capabilities to counter threats. Their intelligence organisation effectiveness gives it an upper hand to not only deal with threats, but pre-empt them before they occur, and have been critical in eliminating leaders of organisations they view a threat to their country.

For example, following the October 7, 2023, Hamas-led attacks on Israel, Prime Minister Benjamin Netanyahu publicly authorised Mossad to pursue Hamas leaders globally. This led to high profile

Figure 2. Comparison Between Armenia's FIS and NSS

	FIS (Foreign Intelligence Service)	NSS (National Security Service)
Primary Mission	External threats and foreign intelligence	Internal security, counter- intelligence, counter-terrorism
Established	October 2023 (newly independent body	Legacy from Soviet-era KGB; evolved after independence
Reports to	Prime Minister of Armenia	Prime Minister of Armenia, but often operates under its own chain
Focus Areas	Political, military, cyber, and economic threats from abroad	Domestic surveillance, anti-corruption, border security
Style	Civilian-led, external-facing	Hybrid civilian-military, internal-facing

assassinations wiping out the Hamas leadership. Israel as a small nation state, surrounded with threats, is a useful example for Armenia on how to pursue intelligence activities aggressively and proactively.

Mossad is considered one of the most effective, feared, and respected intelligence services in the world with a unique combination of strategic culture, national doctrine, elite human resources, and political will.

It has a clear national mission - 'Never Again'. Mossad operates within a national security doctrine shaped by existential threats. Its core mission is to prevent threats before they materialise, and operate globally with a deep moral license from the public and its government. Mossad is an independent organisation reporting directly to the Prime Minister, not through a ministry, which enables fast decision-making, minimal bureaucracy, and agile operations.

It has elite intelligence capabilities known for deep-cover agents, fluent linguists, and cultural infiltration skills. Many operatives are multilingual, trained in acting, psychology, and tradecraft. Recruitment is highly selective, prioritising intellect, resilience, and adaptability over size or rank.

Unlike agencies limited to national borders, Mossad operates anywhere in the world, having a global reach. It operates in the legal grey zones, often conducting extra-judicial killings, kidnappings, sabotage, and surveillance with plausible deniability.

Mossad collaborates with Israel's thriving cyber, AI, and surveillance industries and is an early adopter of emerging technologies, operating hand in glove with the internal intelligence unit Shin Bet. Also, like other effective intelligence organisations, its work overlaps with its global diplomatic presence.

There are two key elements to being able to implement such an organisation. One is budget, which in Israel's case is estimated to be around $3 billion year,[87] legal and policy clarity allowing operational freedom abroad, national security exemptions, and authority for sabotage or assassination under specific threat criteria. Naturally having such a powerful organisation raises concern over its misuse. But if effective and stays core to its mission, it becomes a lethal weapon in a nation's safety and security.

Armenia's predicament is not dissimilar, surrounded by adversaries in Azerbaijan and Turkey, in a volatile region. Faced with catastrophic intelligence failures in the 2020 and 2023 Artsakh wars, Armenia clearly needs to shift from reactive and defensive posture to agile, proactive, intelligence led statecraft.

Armenia's intelligence is going through a transition. Previously, Armenia solely relied on the National Security Service (NSS) which used to handle both internal and foreign intelligence, modelled after the old Soviet KGB. It's focus now is internal affairs.

In 2023, Armenia established its Foreign Intelligence Service (FIS). This civilian agency operates under the direct supervision of the Prime Minister, marking a departure from the Soviet style NSS model. The FIS aims to modernise Armenia's intelligence capabilities, focusing on external threats and aligning more closely with modern intelligence practices.

The FIS is tasked with forecasting, preventing, and countering external threats to Armenia's state and national interests. Its responsibilities encompass the collection and analysis of political, military, economic, and environmental intelligence. The agency emphasises political impartiality and accountability to the public, operating primarily under conditions of secrecy to achieve its objectives. Recent legislative efforts have been made to grant the FIS direct access to state secrets, diminishing the NSS's exclusive control over classified information.

There is some division of responsibilities between the FIS and NSS (listed in table), which can make it counter productive in national intelligence efforts. Given the ongoing transition process, it is anticipated that the legacy National Security Service (NSS) will continue to have its role, authority, and structure evolve, given the rise of the FIS.

In a cruel twist of irony, Armenia published its National Security Strategy in July 2020,[88] just two months prior to its defeat in the Artsakh war of September 2020. The 'National Security Strategy of the Republic of Armenia' was adopted as a guiding document for defining the main directions, threats, challenges, and prioritising security policy.

It's blatantly clear that a new strategy and doctrine is required. As of 2025, efforts are underway for a new draft.[89] A critical element is for Armenia to develop a national intelligence talent pipeline. Armenia is fortunate to have a multilingual population and diaspora.

It needs to iron out the transition process of the NSS and FIS, and be more proactive. The Artsakh war demonstrated that Armenia cannot ever again be compromised on intelligence.

Military Service

For someone who has not served in the military nor sacrificed what many brave Armenians have done so by serving Armenia, this section is particularly difficult to write. One only has to visit Yerablur, Armenia's military cemetery located on a hilltop in the outskirts of Yerevan, or any cemetery in Armenia, to feel the toll and impact war has had on several generations of mainly young men, and women. While the country moves on, those families impacted bear unimaginable pain that stays with them for the rest of their lives.

Given Armenia's precarious national security situation, it is unavoidable not to address this topic.

There remains an environment of anxiousness for parents when their sons and daughters join the military service. The military have a duty of care for service personnel, and they carry a level of responsibility to ensure servicemen and women are not placed knowingly in a vulnerable situation, without adequate support.

There are divergent views on armed forces and its leadership. The armed forces are one of the trusted institutions in the country, yet the leadership is not. In June 2025, a nationwide survey conducted by the US International Republican Institute found that although 72 percent were satisfied or somewhat satisfied with the armed forces, its leadership was at 48 percent.[90]

Armenia has compulsory two year military service for male citizens from the age of 18 to 27, with reserves up to the age of 35. It is the obligation of every male citizen to serve in the military in one form or another. It is estimated that this system only covers only 30 to 40 percent of eligible men.

In 2025, the government introduced reforms to military service, which includes flexible service options with payment alternatives, and extends the maximum conscription age from 27 to 37 years. Among the options is ֏20 million payment in exchange for one month military service, the shortest option available. The extension from 27 to 37 years significantly expands the pool of eligible conscripts, particularly targeting individuals who previously avoided service by

Figure 3. Armenia's Military Service Options

1 month Service	6 months Service	12 months Service	Full Exemption
Ꮱ20M	Ꮱ15M	Ꮱ2.5M	Ꮱ15M
Shortest option	Alternative option	Special category	Citizenship renunciation

aging out of the system. This change is retroactive for certain categories, meaning men currently aged 27 to 37 who haven't completed military service may now be subject to conscription under the new law. In addition, there are several other special provisions and categories. The primary goal of the reforms are to combat widespread draft evasion, generate revenue for state budget, enhance professional army capabilities, and provide legal alternatives to service.

One of the criticisms of the reforms is that they create an inequitable system, where those who can afford it, can significantly reduce their military service.

The Armenian government must also rebuild trust in serving in the military. There are too many horrendous examples in the Artsakh war of 2020, where military positions were left to defend in impossible scenarios. Communication was not always clear. In some instances, soldiers were not equipped to handle technologically advanced drones, nor provided proper equipment or training in a combat zone.

It is a sad reality that service requires readiness to risk one's life, but those who serve should also expect the best possible means to defend themselves and their colleagues. This demands investment in equipment, training, and strong leadership.

Multiple measures are required to rebuild trust for those serving in the military including increased transparency and accountability measures, and open communication with the public. Exaggerated or misleading information erodes trust. Having clear ethical guidelines for military personnel, strong enforcement measures in combating corruption in the military, and significant and sizeable investment in modern military technology with effective training – will all go towards rebuilding trust.

Chapter Five

Improved Governance

Unfinished Business of Combating Corruption

No Smart Nation can succeed without a solid governance foundation and a framework that eliminates corruption. Though Armenia has taken steps to improve governance, including addressing corruption, this effort requires constant vigilance. Corruption in Armenia continues to exist.

It is a structural legacy. For decades, opaque governance, patronage networks, and institutional weaknesses have allowed corruption to entrench itself as a parallel system of power. The 2018 Velvet Revolution resulted in a change of government and Nikol Pashinyan coming to power. It disrupted the political status quo. Yet the deeper battle — that of building resilient, transparent, and citizen-centric institutions — remains ongoing.

The Anti-Corruption Committee reported an increase in corruption-related offenses, with 1,088 cases recorded in the first nine months of 2023, a 79.5 percent rise compared to the same period in 2022,[91] which could imply enhanced detection and reporting mechanisms.

The Transparency International 2024 report ranks Armenia 63rd out of 180 countries.[92] An improvement since the first edition of Smart Nation where it ranked 95th (out of 168 countries). Transparency International is a global non-governmental organisation that combats corruption.

Armenia's score of 47 in the Corruptions Perception Index is higher than the global average of 43. The higher the score, the better your ranking, and although Armenia is now better than average, it still has much to address. Transparency International's Ccorruption Perception's Index has small states dominating the top of the list with Denmark ranked 1st, followed by Finland, Singapore, New Zealand, Luxembourg, Norway, Switzerland, Sweden, and Netherlands.

The United Nations Development Program (UNDP) views corruption as one of the major governance challenges in Armenia but acknowledges progress in recent years, especially through the establishment of the Anti-Corruption Committee in 2021, the creation of specialised anti-corruption courts in 2022, and the adoption of comprehensive anti-corruption strategies. The UNDP frames Armenia as a 'country in transition', from systemic corruption toward institutional integrity. Its regional governance report viewed Armenia's anti-corruption reforms as important progress, but achieving irreversible change would require deep institutional resilience and public trust in independent oversight mechanisms.

Corruption today is less visible but more elusive. It has shifted from overt to subtler forms, conflict of interest in public-private partnerships, regulatory capture, and influence over judicial decisions.

Armenia's 2023–2026 Anti-Corruption Strategy is an ambitious blueprint. It promises to institutionalise integrity across the public sector, digitise services to minimise human discretion, and establish autonomous oversight bodies. Key pillars include the establishment of the Anti-Corruption Committee, asset declaration and monitoring, digitisation of public services, and public procurement reform using transparent digital platforms and competitive bidding processes. The Anti-Corruption Policy Council, chaired by the Prime Minister, oversees the strategy's execution, ensuring coordination among various stakeholders

Reform is only part of the equation, execution is the real test. Institutional resistance, capacity gaps, and political ambivalence have slowed implementation. Many reforms rely on executive goodwill rather than legal enforcement. Meanwhile, civil society, a vital accountability actor, remains underfunded and occasionally sidelined.

The absence of high-profile prosecutions or effective asset recovery cases signals to the public that impunity may still prevail. Moreover, without parallel judicial reform, anti-corruption bodies risk becoming isolated actors in a compromised legal ecosystem.

If Armenia is to become a Smart Nation, it must embed integrity not as a compliance box but as a design principle across its governance architecture. That requires reimagining anti-corruption not merely as enforcement but as a cornerstone of innovation and competitiveness.

Some additional initiatives for consideration could include data oversight, deploy AI to detect anomalies in procurement, budgeting, and administrative processes, and pattern recognition can become Armenia's greatest ally in early detection of corruption; integrity by design, shift from reliance on whistleblowers and audits to embedding transparency into systems such as real-time publication of government contracts; independent judiciary, the judiciary's budget and governance should be protected from political manipulation; and leadership by example, anti-corruption begins at the top, full transparency of income and assets, and zero tolerance for nepotism.

Armenia's future hinges on its ability to earn and sustain the trust of its citizens. Corruption is not just a moral issue, it is an economic, security, and statehood issue. Institutional credibility is a strategic asset. The fight against corruption is won by building institutions that function predictably, transparently, and equitably, institutions that outlast governments and serve citizens.

e-Goverment

A remarkable development has been the progress of e-Government services across Armenia. In the first edition of Smart Nation, it was recommended that each citizen has a digital identity to allow the full complement of digital government services, modelled on Estonia.

In 2016, Armenia ranked 87th out of 193 countries in the UN e-Government Development Index. In 2024, Armenia was ranked 48th.[93] The report noted the Armenian government's prioritisation of digital transformation, and establishment of a national data governance framework. Other developments noted include a unified e-government services platform, a cybersecurity excellence centre, an electronic tax filing system, and an e-health portal.

Armenia has also adopted a national digital identity system called YesEm (translates to 'It's me'), designed as a secure, single signon solution across public and private sector digital services. YesEm is Armenia's state digital identity platform, launched in December 2023 for government e-services. In January 2024, all digital government services were required to go through YesEm. Operated by the Information Systems Agency of Armenia, YesEm provides a unified authentication gateway and supports digital signatures compliant with eIDAS 2.0, EU's regulation for electronic identification, authentication and trust services.

Yerevan is also littered with self-service kiosks operated by organisations like Tel-Cell, EasyPay and iDram. Services provide citizens with a one-stop shop to pay utility bills, government payments, with users receiving a receipt confirming the transaction. There are also app based options for a complete digital experience.

In 2025, this was complemented by imID, a trust service provider backed by banks and telecoms, which enhance authentication, digital signatures, and secure document exchange for both public and private services. These steps have positioned Armenia to deliver more seamless, cross-border compatible digital services, laying the foundation for a modern data-driven public sector.

The next evolution is better leveraging data to help make improved public policy decisions. By analysing data effectively, policymakers can identify trends, predict future challenges, understand the root causes of problems, and develop evidence-based solutions that improve the efficiency and efficacy of public services. It also puts an onus on Ministries when requesting funding, that it be evidence and data based.

It also places an obligation on Ministries to ensure that funding requests are evidence and data based.

The Armenian government's data.gov.am is an open data portal providing public access to various government datasets, however, usage is fragmented and not fully integrated across ministries. The Statistical Committee of Armenia collects demographic, social, and economic data, which is used for some evidence-based policymaking (e.g, social protection program), but integration is limited.

A small state that has efficiently leveraged data for enhanced public policy decisions is Estonia. Estonia's X-Road platform allows government agencies to securely exchange data. The platform provides access to real-time data - creating a secure, auditable digital infrastructure that promotes innovation and citizen trust. During

COVID-19, Estonia was able to quickly cross-reference health and population data to manage testing and vaccination efficiently through the effective use of data and its platform.

Armenia needs to leverage this capability for improved public policy decisions and outcomes.

Cost of Living

According to the Cost of Living Index by City 2025,[94] Yerevan is the most expensive city in the South Caucasus. In fact, based on 2025 figures, it is marginally higher than Istanbul and many other cities in Turkey. A rise in cost of living is due to numerous factors including rent, driven by housing demand, and overall living expenses. Out of 404 cities in the Index, it was ranked 257, and in recent years has been rising in rankings.

Cost of Living increases are influenced by many factors, and not always negative – for example, it can also be attributed to higher wages, or a strong national currency.

Another factor was Russian migration to Armenia during the Russia-Ukraine conflict combined with sanctions placed on Russia. By November 2022, an estimated 55,000 people had arrived from Russia, corresponding to around 1.8 percent of the total Armenian population.[95] In 2022, rents in Yerevan surged 30-40 percent influenced by this factor.[96] The relocation wave contributed to a consumption increase of around 2.6 percent in 2023, creating both a short-term economic stimulus and inflationary pressure.[97] Furthermore, an estimated 77 percent of migrants came from high-skilled jobs, providing them higher disposable incomes.

Since the last edition of Smart Nation, the Armenian currency, the dram has appreciated in value against the US dollar by around 20-25 percent, which means increasing purchasing power. As of June 2025, average monthly nominal wages in Armenia were around ֏357,950.[98]

Yerevan is a more expensive city to visit, live and work in than before and that adds certain pressure points to the Armenian economy.

One of the measures the Armenian government has undertaken is to increase spending to mitigate the rise in living costs. In 2025, the Armenian government set aside approximately ֏905billion for social protection, an increase of nearly 15 percent over 2024. That amounts to around 8.2 percent of GDP.[99] Despite rising social spending, pension increases lag behind living costs.

The Armenian government arguably has more funding at its disposal, given it no longer funds Artsakh. It was estimated around 75 percent of Artsakh's State budget was provided by Armenia,[100] upwards of $250 million annually. Some of that would have been redirected to settling refugees in Armenia.

Addressing cost of living issues is not a simple fix. It is often influenced by global factors such as inflation and geopolitical crises, as well as local issues. Yerevan in particular needs to be careful that cost of living does not escalate to the point where it can detrimentally impact the local population, as well as impacting international visitors who are often seeking value for money and can be price conscious. However, it is a good thing for Armenia's economy that it is not competing to attract foreign tourists based on price but what it has on offer.

The Armenian government can only leverage its natural assets and provide targeted spending measures in order to address cost of living issues, whether it be around energy, water, and other infrastructure projects that can materially impact the local population.

Chapter Six

Stimulating Growth – the Next Economic Chapter

When seeking to grow the economy, a diversified economy is a valuable indicator. The Economic Complexity Index (ECI) is a measure of how diversified and sophisticated a country's export structure is. It reflects not just how many different products a country exports, but also how unique or complex those products are. Higher ECI scores correlate with higher potential for economic growth because such economies have more productive capabilities, knowledge accumulation, and adaptability.

According to the most recent rankings of 2023, Armenia was ranked as the 58th most complex economy. This suggests Armenia is mid-level in terms of complexity globally, with room to diversify. Compared to other small nation states like Singapore, Finland, Israel, Denmark, and Estonia, all of whom are ranked with the top 30. This is something Armenia should aspire and aim towards.

Tourism

Tourism continues to grow in Armenia, attracting more than two million visitors every year. The largest number of tourists to Armenia come from Russia (around 42.5 percent), Georgia (around 12 percent) and Iran (around 8 percent) – one of the highest growing influx.[101]

Other countries in sequential order include the United States, India, China, France, Germany, Ukraine, the Philippines, Belarus, Italy, the Netherlands, the Republic of Korea, Turkey, the United Kingdom, Poland, and Kazakhstan. Plans are underway to attract three million tourists by the end of the decade.[102]

Armenia continues to attract interest as a travel destination. Armenia was featured in Lonely Planet's 'Best in Travel 2025' list, highlighting its blend of natural beauty, historical significance, and cultural richness. This inclusion positions Armenia among the top travel destinations recommended for exploration.[103] Also in the same year, BBC produced '*Sunrise in Armenia*' featured in Paramount Pictures' international television programming, attracting millions of viewers.

In 2024, *National Geographic* featured an article on Armenia titled, 'Why Armenia Should Be on Your Radar in 2024,' emphasising Armenia's year-round appeal, spotlighting its vibrant wine culture, scenic hiking trails, and rich cultural heritage.[104]

Armenia's natural beauty beyond its capital is an asset. It can be argued that it has one of the best hiking trails anywhere in the world, with well-marked trails across the country. Armenia has UNESCO world heritage sites, including the cathedral and churches of Etchmiadzin, Armenia's religious headquarters, the archaeological site of Zvartnots, the monastery of Geghard in the Upper Azat Valley, and the monasteries of Haghpat and Sanahin, located in Armenia's north, near Alaverdi.

Some potential tourism landmarks remain stagnant. One of the most symbolic is the incompletion of the Cascade located in Yerevan. The complex, which houses the Cafesjian Center for the Arts, includes terraced gardens leading to a staircase to Victory Monument (commemorating Armenians who served in the Second World War), and provides spectacular views of Mount Ararat and Yerevan. The completion of the project has faced numerous delays. The concept of the Cascade was first proposed by architect Alexander Tamanyan, who worked on the project of modern Yerevan in the 1920's. In 1970, 34 years after Alexander Tamanyan's death, the Soviet Union returned to the idea of building the Cascade. The Soviet authorities allocated the funds with some changes to the original plan. Construction started in the 1980's but was interrupted shortly afterwards.

Then in 2002, the Cafesjian Museum Foundation (led by philanthropist Gerard Cafesjian) took control and invested over $35 million to restore and open the Cafesjian Museum of Art in 2009. However, this only completed the lower portions of the Cascade, the upper terraces and connection to the Victory Monument remained missing. Yerevan city have indicated that they would not finance the upper section. Instead, the project was to be carried out by private investment secure in development rights. The Yerevan authorities have awarded the long-awaited completion of the city's iconic Cascade complex to a local developer. The winning bid includes a $52 million investment, which will finally realise architect Alexander Tamanyan's vision after decades of the landmark remaining unfinished.[105]

It is almost inconceivable that any other government administration would take so long to revitalise a project so impactful on tourism.

Regional Tourism

One of the recommendations in the last edition of Smart Nation was developing and implementing a regional tourism plan – and there has been some notable progress.

Armenia is actively developing its regional tourism through a Tourism and Regional Infrastructure Project (TRIP)[106] focused on seven key clusters. The goal is to improve infrastructure, enhance tourism offerings, and promote sustainable and inclusive growth in areas like Areni, Dilijan, Dvin, Gyumri, Jermuk, Goris, and Yeghegis. This project, funded by the European Bank for Reconstruction and Development (EBRD) and the Armenian government at a cost of €120.5 million, is implemented by Armenia's Territorial Development Fund and aims to boost tourism and regional development across Armenia by 2030.

They focus on key areas unique to those region. For example, Areni focuses on wine tourism, leveraging the region's vineyards and winemaking traditions; Dilijan emphasises ecotourism and adventure tourism, with Dilijan National Park offering forests, rivers, and mineral springs; Dvin explores the historical and cultural significance of the area; Gyumri has cultural and educational tourism as the focus, highlighting the city's rich history and architectural heritage; Jermuk aims to develop its potential as a wellness and resort destination; Goris focuses on promoting cultural heritage tourism, showcasing the region's historical sites and unique landscapes; and Yeghegis promotes adventure tourism and outdoor activities.

This is a significant milestone and will help maximise economic and job creation opportunities in Armenia's regions.

Visa Reforms

Armenia has been actively implementing visa reforms to boost tourism. In 2025, changes included visa-free entry for citizens of several countries, including from the GCC (Gulf Cooperation Council) and other nations like Australia, New Zealand, Singapore, and South Korea. These reforms aim to simplify entry for tourists and encourage travel to Armenia.

Armenia already has visa-free regimes with many other countries, including the US, Japan, and countries from the CIS.

In June 2025, Armenia and EU officials finalised a Visa Liberalisation Action Plan, setting a roadmap toward visa-free access for Armenian citizens to the Schengen area. A Schengen visa is a short-stay visa that allows individuals to travel within the Schengen Area for up to 90 days within a 180 day period. It grants access to 26 European countries without border controls between them.

Armenia aims to introduce biometric passports by 2026, one of the key benchmarks for the EU. One area for potential consideration is introducing multilateral visa schemes with Georgia and Iran (similar to the Schengen model) to promote multi-country tours in the Caucasus, and certain neighbouring countries.

Airline Connectivity

Armenia has had a chequered history of national carriers and national branded airlines. Since the collapse of Armavia (Armenia's last national airline, ceased in 2013), the government has pursued an 'open skies' liberal aviation policy, encouraging private and foreign-owned carriers to operate freely in Armenia.

Armenian Airlines is dormant, established in December 2022 and unrelated to the former state-owned flag carrier by the same name. In April 2025, the airline suspended all flights due to the renewal of its fleet and the acquisition of new aircraft. In May 2025, the Armenian Civil Aviation Committee suspended the airlines Air Operator Certificate due to the carrier having no airworthy aircraft in its fleet.

In 2021, FlyOne Armenia was founded as a subsidiary of Moldovan carrier FlyOne and is regarded Armenia's flagship low-cost airline based at Zvartnots International Airport in Yerevan. FlyOne Armenia has expanded to more than 25 destinations, including Paris, Milan, Dubai, Tbilisi, and Tel Aviv.

One of the major factors positively impacting on the number of tourists in Armenia is the larger number of direct flights to Yerevan. This also provides an opportunity for Armenians within Armenia to access international travel more than ever before.

It is estimated that direct flights have enabled a near tripling of annual tourist arrivals (from around 500,000 in 2014 to over 1.6 million in 2023). All airports in Armenia receive flights from 70 airports in 29 countries, operated by 36 different airlines, including 12 low-cost carriers. [107] This is a marked increase from a decade ago.

In May 2025, low-cost airline WizzAir announced its 34th base in Yerevan, launching eight new routes across six countries, connecting Armenia to more of Europe than ever before. Certain segments, such as tourism from Gulf countries (UAE, Qatar, Saudi Arabia), have increased after visa waivers and direct connections. The increased number of indirect connections have also helped with new cargo routes.

One significant opportunity yet to be realised are direct flights from one of the largest diaspora communities – the United States to Armenia. In September 2024, Armenia's Deputy Minister announced ongoing government discussions to launch direct routes from Yerevan to Los Angeles and New York, pending legal and EU overflight arrangements. [108] Direct US flights would enhance economic links under the 2025 Armenia–US Strategic Partnership Charter. [109]

The causes for the delay are various. Before an airline can launch US service, authorities must inspect and certify Armenian airports and airline procedures. This process can be lengthy and Armenia's airport safety oversight was flagged previously (there was a partial EU ban on airlines in 2020), suggesting ongoing modernisation and regulatory improvements are still in progress.

Both US and Armenian officials stress that route decisions are based primarily on commercial viability, and airlines need demonstration of consistent passenger demand and profitability. While there is interest, there's limited official market data proving sustained demand.

In addition to meeting compliance requirements, the Armenian government could consider partnering with the American Chamber Commerce of Armenia and providing a report on the viability and economic opportunity a direct route may bring. This would be beneficial to any prospective airline, as well as Armenia's economy.

Cargo Logistics

Armenia has been actively working to position itself as a regional cargo and logistics hub, particularly in the South Caucasus and between Europe, the Middle East, and Asia. While it's still developing, Armenia has made some strides in infrastructure, regulatory reform, and international partnerships to enhance its cargo connectivity.

Some notable infrastructure projects include the North-South Road Corridor, creating a fast, modern highway connecting Iran to Georgia via Armenia. Several sections were completed with financing from the Asian Development Bank (ADB) and European Investment Bank (EIB). This provides a key trade route from the Persian Gulf to the Black Sea.

Zvartnots International Airport Yerevan has an expanded cargo terminal. According to 2023 estimates, this airport handles more than 22,000 tons of cargo per year. It has cold chain capabilities to handle perishables and pharmaceuticals.

It is worth noting that Emirates SkyCargo, the air freight division of Emirates is considered the fourth largest cargo airline worldwide in terms of the total freight tonne-kilometres flown and international freight tonne-kilometres flown.[110] With Dubai-Yerevan being only a three hour flight, there is significant potential to leverage this hub, not only for Armenian perishable exports, but also Yerevan becoming a bespoke regional hub.

The Meghri Free Economic Zone which borders Iran is designed to serve as a gateway for Iran-EEU trade, details of which were earlier mentioned in the book.

Armenia can accelerate efforts to become a regional cargo hub through rapid completion of the North-South Corridor, upgrading Gyumri Airport for low-cost air cargo, modernising customs with full paperless processing, and fully implementing the Meghri free economic zone – with incentives for logistics firms to promote Armenia as a Cold Chain Gateway for Iran-CIS-Europe perishables, and public-private partnerships with global logistics leaders (eg, DHL, Maersk, DB Schenker).

Medical Tourism

Globally there is an emergence of medical tourism, where people from Western economies travel to certain parts of the world to have cosmetic or medical procedures which are far cheaper than in their own country. This presents Armenia with a significant opportunity.

It is estimated that Armenia's medical tourism is valued at more than $250 million a year. To put this into perspective, Turkey's medical tourism is estimated between $2.5–3 billion a year and globally recognised as a destination for hair transplants.

Medical procedures in Armenia typically cost between 40-70 percent less than in Western countries. For example, a dental implant that could cost up to $4,000 in the United States might be performed for as little as $1,000 in Armenia.[111]

Armenia's Ministry of Economy and Tourism Committee is collaborating with the Ministry of Health, to develop special programs to support the growing sector.

While rhinoplasty and dentistry remain the most popular services, other areas are expanding rapidly. Body contouring procedures are gaining traction, and Armenia's cardiac surgery and haematology deserve recognition for their excellence. The combination of skilled practitioners, competitive pricing, comprehensive service packages, and the opportunity to explore Armenia's rich cultural heritage creates a compelling proposition for medical tourists. It is an emerging industry in which Armenia has a competitive advantage and should leverage to its full potential.

Investment

Armenia's investment policies can be described as liberal, open, and increasingly reform-oriented, with a focus on attracting foreign direct investment (FDI), supporting innovation, and integrating with global markets.

Foreign investors can fully own businesses without local partners. Repatriation of profits and capital is allowed with few restrictions. In the World Bank's 'Doing Business' 2020 report, Armenia was ranked 47th out of 190 countries. This ranking reflects the ease of starting and operating a business in Armenia compared to other countries.

Armenia's laws on foreign investment guarantees equal rights for foreign and domestic investors, protection from nationalisation/ expropriation without compensation, and right to access courts and international arbitration. Armenia has more than 40 bilateral investment treaties signed, including with France, China, Germany, Russia, and the US.

Armenia is a member of the EEU, which allows duty-free access to more than a 180 million person market. Armenia has been a member of the World Trade Organisation since 2003, with low average tariffs, and is signatory to the Comprehensive and Enhanced Partnership Agreement with the EU, committing to regulatory alignment and solid governance.

There are some sensitive or strategic sectors where foreign ownership or participation is limited, regulated, or subject to approval. These include national security and defence, energy, and telecommunications.

Under Armenian law, foreign ownership of broadcast media companies is restricted, and limits may apply to direct or indirect foreign control of television or radio stations.

Foreign nationals cannot own agricultural land; however, they can lease agricultural land long-term (up to 99 years). Foreign legal entities can acquire urban and industrial land, and agricultural land only via registered Armenian subsidiaries.

Armenia could benefit from a more calibrated approach to FDI. Small states – especially those with limited markets, security concerns, or geographic constraints like Armenia – must be strategise to attract foreign investment.

Successful small countries use a combination of regulatory innovation, niche specialisation, and strong branding to overcome scale disadvantages. Armenia can learn from other small states in attracting further investment.

Singapore's Economic Development Board is the country's investment attracting arm. It is one of the world's most effective investment promotion agencies. It plays a central, strategic role in attracting FDI, particularly in high-value, future-oriented sectors.

EDB doesn't promote everything, it focuses on future ready sectors, such as advanced manufacturing; semiconductors, pharmaceuticals and biotech, clean energy and green tech, digital and AI services, and financial technology. It identifies global trends early and positions Singapore as a base for multinational companies (MNCs) to serve the Asia Pacific region. EDB maintains a network of overseas offices in key markets, such as US, Germany, Japan, China, India, and works as a deal-maker and advisor, not just a bureaucratic body. EDB officers often function like consultants for major corporations. EDB offers 'concierge-style' facilitation for major investors with end-to-end support, permits, land, talent sourcing, and regulatory navigation, and it connects companies to universities, research and development grants, and workforce training.

The result is that Singapore consistently ranks in the top five in the World Bank's 'Ease of Doing Business,' and among the world's largest FDI inflow per capita. It hosts 37,000 international companies, including 4,000 regional headquarters of multinationals.

Another example is the United Arab Emirates. As of 2020–2021, the UAE has allowed 100 percent foreign ownership of mainland (onshore) companies in most sectors. This removed the previous requirement of having a 51 percent local Emirati partner, making the UAE far more attractive to global investors.

The UAE has over 40 free zones offering very low corporate and personal income tax, 100 percent foreign ownership, full repatriation of profits and capital, no customs duties on imports/exports within the zones, and simplified licensing and regulation. Like Singapore, it uses targeted sector policies to promote investment. In the 2020 World Bank's 'Ease of Doing Business' report, UAE achieved a rank of 16th overall.

Another small state which has succeeded in attracting inbound investment is Ireland. Benefiting from the UK's Brexit and leaving the EU, it has positioned itself as a low tax haven, and a location that has talent that can support multinational companies. Ireland's has a small population of just over five million people.

The Irish model combines fiscal incentives, EU access, a skilled workforce, and institutional agility, backed by proactive promotion through its Ireland Foreign Direct Investment Agency (IDA). In the World Bank's 'Ease of Doing Business' report, Ireland is ranked 24th out of 190 economies.

Ireland focuses on strategic, high-value sectors including ICT and software (Google, Apple, Facebook have EU headquarters in Ireland), pharmaceuticals and medtech, Financial services & fintech Data centres, AI and advanced manufacturing.

Ireland offers a 12.5 percent corporate tax rate, one of the lowest in the OECD, while it joined the OECD global minimum tax 15 percent agreement. It is one of the few EU countries with English as the primary business language, and it attracts talent from across Europe due to quality of life, multinational presence, and talent visa schemes.

As an EU member, Ireland offers barrier-free access to the entire EU single market, which is around 450 million people. Like Singapore's EDB, the IDA provides concierge-level investor services such as site selection, workforce planning, and permits.

Enterprise Armenia, the official national investment promotion agency, operates under the Ministry of Economy and serves as a 'one-stop shop' to attract, support, and retain both domestic and foreign investments. Compared to world-leading agencies like Ireland's IDA or Singapore EDB. Enterprise Armenia is smaller in capacity and reach (limited overseas offices or in-market deal teams), and less digitised—processes are not yet fully automated or transparent online.

Armenia is making efforts to stand out from other competing markets in attracting investment. It offers a talented workforce producing 4,000 ICT graduates annually, competitive salaries estimated to be one third of Western Europe or the United States, with high productivity, and the benefit of local and repatriates returning to Armenia supporting multiple languages for customer support.

Armenia has free trade access to the EEU and EU, providing tariff-free access to around 6,000 goods, and a preferential trade arrangement with Iran. One of very few countries with preferential access to both Russia and EU.

Armenia has more than 30 percent of its energy already from renewables (hydro, solar), which is particular attractive to some multinationals who want to offset their carbon emissions. Armenia's solar irradiation is among the highest in Europe and competitive energy pricing. It also has a corporate income tax of 18 percent, which is competitive.

Enterprise Armenia could learn from other small nation investment agencies and how they have successfully implemented their unique qualities to become an attractive investment destination. The table below provides Enterprise Armenia offerings, other small states cited provide the full breadth of services.

Public Transport

Improved public transport could play a critical role in improving Armenia's economic growth. This section will focus on Armenia's capital Yerevan with a population of more than a million people and a third of the country's population. With the greater use of private transport vehicles, the capital is under increased strain and congestion.

Over 90 percent of public transport passengers rely on buses or minibuses (*marshrutkas*). Since 2022, over 300 new compressed natural gas and diesel Euro 6 standard buses were introduced as part of Yerevan's ongoing fleet reform.

Yerevan's metro system consists of ten stations and is 13.4 kilometres long. Though clean and reliable, it only services part of the

Figure 4. Enterprise Armenia Offerings

Feature/Service	Enterprise Armenia
One stop shop model	✔
Overseas offices/investor reach	⚠
Tailored investor onboarding	⚠
Permit and regulatory facilitation	⚠
Aftercare services	⚠
Incentive navigation	✔
Investor visa/residency support	⚠
Digital platforms and data tools	⚠
Strategic sector promoted	✔

✔ Offered   ⚠ Limited/developing

city needs. Yerevan has planned to expand its metro system, with the construction of Ajapnyak station. This will be the 11th station in the Yerevan metro, expected to serve a densely populated area. The project is estimated to cost $50 million, with $24.6 million allocated in the 2025 state budget. Construction is scheduled to start in 2026.

In order to relieve some of the congestion, Yerevan has introduced paid parking zones, implemented primarily in central Yerevan (Kentron district), but plans to extend to surrounding districts (eg, Arabkir, Nor Nork). In January 2025, Yerevan implemented a unified ticket system, which means cash payments are no longer accepted on buses and the metro.

Yerevan is also prioritising dedicated lanes for public transportation. A unified corridor will connect several administrative districts, ensuring unobstructed public transit flow. The corridor will extend from the Kentron district toward Arshakunyats, Garegin

Figure 5. Twelve Districts of Yerevan

Figure 6: Yerevan Metro

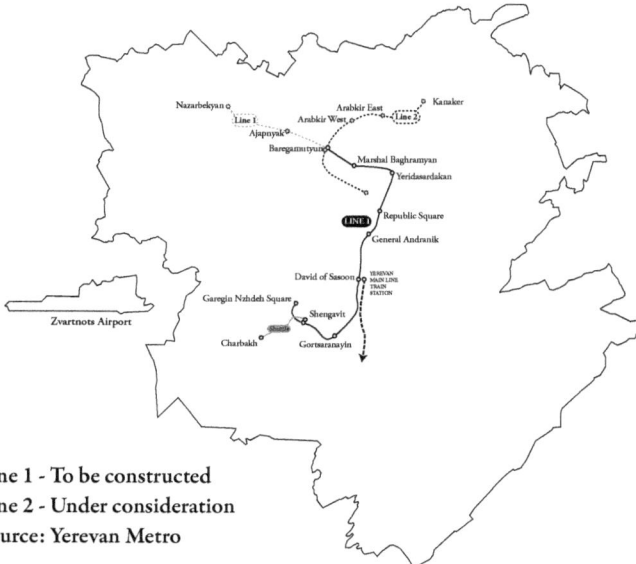

Line 1 - To be constructed
Line 2 - Under consideration
Source: Yerevan Metro

Nzhdeh, and Bagratunyats streets. Work is underway to connect the Nor Nork district to Arabkir and extend access to Malatia-Sebastia.[112] There are dedicated bus lanes on Abovyan, Moskovyan, Isahakyan, and Saralanj streets, as well as on Mashtots Avenues, ensuring buses maintain their schedules to optimise traffic flow.

Despite all these steps, congestion remains and is worsening. Yerevan needs to expedite its Metro masterplan and beyond Ajapnyak, have it better funded, expand it to Zvartnots airport and other parts of Yerevan, where population density is becoming an issue. The metro removes vehicles from streets, improves air quality, and is a fast and reliable form of transportation. This type of project can transform the city, bringing significant economic benefits and put Yerevan among other small smart cities.

Chapter Seven

Smart Management of Natural Resources

Towards Responsible Mining

For a small state, Armenia has considerable mineral wealth, which forms an important segment of its economy. In 2023, the sector accounted for 2.7 percent of GDP, with exports accounting for $2.8 billion or 37 percent of total exports,[113] and accounted for 6.8 percent of government revenues in 2022.[114] It is estimated the sector employs more than 11,000 people.[115]

Armenia is a major producer of molybdenum which is used in high quality forms of steel and other alloys. Armenia has significant deposits of copper and gold, smaller deposits of lead, silver and zinc, and deposits of industrial minerals including basalt, diatomite, granite, gypsum, limestone and perlite. Although mining has brought sizeable economic benefits, it has led to some environmental impacts. These impacts span from air and water pollution, deforestation, and soil degradation to threats to biodiversity and public health.

The Teghut mine in Lori Province caused the destruction of over 350 hectares of forest during its open-pit copper mining operation. This resulted in ecosystem loss, erosion, and loss of habitat for endemic species. The mine was temporarily shut down in 2018 due to tailings dam concerns (a tailing dam is a structure used to impound and store waste materials left over after the processing of mined ore). Mines discharge untreated water containing arsenic, cadmium, lead, and other toxic metals into rivers like Debed, Voghji, and Akhuryan. The Akhtala tailings pond was found to be leaking into nearby farmland and Debed river. Contamination has affected drinking water supplies and aquatic life.[116]

Mining operations generate particulate matter like dust, and release sulfur dioxide and nitrogen oxides, and heavy metals into the air, especially near processing facilities. Smelting operations in Alaverdi historically caused heavy pollution. Dust from tailings dams has affected air quality in Kajaran, Kapan, and Ararat. More than 25 tailings dams in Armenia store toxic sludge, and most are poorly regulated and lack sufficient safeguards against seismic risk, critical in an earthquake-prone region. The Amulsar gold mine attracted concerns due to potential cyanide use in heap leaching and its proximity to Lake Sevan, Armenia's main freshwater reserve. Villagers near mines (eg Kajaran, Alaverdi, Shnogh) report increased rates of respiratory illness, skin disease, contaminated drinking water, and reduced crop yields. Residents in Jermuk, near the Amulsar mine, led a multi-year protest citing health concerns and risk to tourism.[117]

Armenia has taken steps to reform its mining sector, but serious gaps remain in enforcement, environmental protection, community rights, and sustainable development. In addition, organisations like the Mining Legislation Reform Institute (MLRI) have been formed with the goal of making mining in Armenia responsible by clarifying the legal obligations of mining companies and making them legally binding. The MLRI was founded in 2014 as a department of the Responsible Mining Centre of the American University of Armenia, and in 2019 it became an independent non-profit organisation, funded by the Tufenkyan Foundation.

In 2017, Armenia was formally admitted to the Extractive Industries Transparency Initiative (EITI). The initiative is a global standard to promote the open and accountable management of natural resources. The composition of Armenia's multi-stakeholder group is chaired by Armenia's Deputy Prime Minister and includes representatives from government, mining companies, and civil society. In a positive development, in 2024, it secured an 89.5/100 score from EITI demonstrating collaboration between government, civil society and companies, robust data disclosures, and tangible progress in turning transparency into policy reforms and impact.

In 2024, the Armenian government adopted new regulations implementing changes to the law governing the Environmental Impact Assessment (EIA) process, including the mining sector, making the mining license application and approval processes scientifically based, thereby reducing the discretion of mining enterprises when presenting information on geological data and impact on vital ecosystems. By incorporating EIA reports as part of

Figure 7. Armenia's Mining Practices

Reform	Stage
EITI membership	✔
Mining license transparency	✔
Environmental assessments	⚠
Tailing dam standards	⚠
Community rights	⚠
Mine closure rules	✕
Monitoring/enforcement	⚠
Green mining incentives	✕

✔ Approved   ⚠ In progress/requires further development   ✕ Not approved

the mining license application process, the new rules will make companies accountable for the environmental commitments outlined in their EIA reports.

Despite progress, there are areas that still require reforms to bring Armenia to the forefront of responsible mining, such as adopting enforceable mine closure laws, conducting a national tailings safety audit, creating a 'Green Mining Certification' system for responsible mining, establishing a national Mine Rehabilitation Fund, and ensuring that real-time environmental monitoring is mandatory for all operating mines.

Water: A Strategic Resource

Armenia's water resources are a strategic asset vital for agriculture, energy, drinking water, and ecosystems. It is a valuable resource and commodity of which Armenia has an abundance. Armenia is water-rich per capita for the region, but can do much better to manage it efficiently, and treat it as a valuable asset.

A distinct and recognisable feature in Armenia is the water drinking fountains called pulpulak (Armenian: պուլպուլակ). Pulpulaks are a significant part of Armenian culture and first appeared on the streets of Yerevan in the 1920's. Pulpulaks are small, usually one metre tall, made from stone with running water, often fed by a mountain spring. Their endless supply of fresh drinking water, embody Armenia's abundance of this natural resource.

Small nation-states like Singapore, Israel, and the UAE would envy the natural water supply that Armenia enjoys. While Armenia does not export bulk water, it derives economic returns from hydropower, agriculture, bottled water, and tourism—making water a de facto national export commodity. Yet its management remains fragmented.

It is estimated that around 70 percent of water is used for irrigation and the remaining 30 percent for hydropower producing electricity. As with any strategic asset careful management is required. Challenges remain with Armenia's water supply including: Ararat Valley aquifer is dangerously depleted; some rivers are contaminated, whether it be sewage, mining or agricultural waste; Lake Sevan has experienced stress with water level drops due to hydropower releases; inefficient irrigation with much outdated infrastructure, estimating up to 60 percent of water lost in transit; as well as climate change impacting river flows.

There are several reforms required to better manage this critical resource, including installing smart meters across irrigation and municipal systems. Smart meters help shift water management from a reactive, inefficient, and opaque system to one that is data-driven, accountable, and sustainable. A case in point is stopping illegal wells. An estimated 2,000 illegal wells and unmetered withdrawals in Ararat and Armavir have led to severe groundwater depletion, with aquifers dropping more than ten metres. Smart meters enable real-time tracking of how much water is being drawn, by whom, and when, and allows the enforcement of extraction limits and early detection of overuse, helping to stabilise aquifer levels.

Armenia loses up to 60 percent of irrigation water due to leaks, outdated canals, and inefficient flood irrigation. Smart meters installed at farm gates and distribution points track actual use and flow losses. Data helps target repairs, optimise delivery, and enable transition to drip irrigation, which can double water productivity.

Current water pricing is a flat rate, often based on estimated use, not actual consumption, leading to waste. Smart meters allow for tiered or volumetric pricing, charging more for excess use and incentivising conservation, as well as improving cost recovery for water systems and ensuring equitable access for all users.

Lack of real usage data makes it hard to plan new infrastructure or climate adaptation strategies. Smart meters generate high-resolution usage data, which can be analysed by region, sector, and season, and helps policymakers prioritise investment in infrastructure.

Israel provides an important case study in water efficiency. Necessary, given it has a harsh desert climate, limited freshwater supply, and a need to support agriculture for national food security, smart metering has played a central role in water management. The country implemented smart water meters across its entire agricultural sector, enabling real-time monitoring of irrigation at the plot level. These meters are integrated with remote sensing and weather data to optimise when and how much water is used. Farmers receive alerts on mobile apps, and water authorities can detect leaks, unauthorised use, and inefficiencies instantly. This system helped Israel reduce agricultural water use by over 30 percent while increasing crop yields.[118] This system underpins its globally competitive agri-tech export sector.

Another meaningful reform that can and should be delivered is drip irrigation. Drip irrigation, also known as trickle irrigation, is a method of watering that delivers water slowly and directly to the plant's root zone. It involves using a network of tubes, pipes, and emitters to distribute water drop by drop, minimising water waste, loss from evaporation and maximising efficiency. This technique is particularly beneficial for agriculture. Drip irrigation uses 30–50 percent less water than conventional methods, making it ideal for over-extracted regions like the Ararat Valley, where aquifers are being dangerously depleted.

Drip irrigation improves crop yields by up to 40–70 percent and enhances quality by maintaining consistent moisture. This is especially valuable for high-value crops like grapes, apricots, berries, and tomatoes—key Armenian exports.

Armenia faces increasing climate volatility, with less snow, hotter summers, and more frequent droughts. Drip systems allow precision irrigation, reducing vulnerability to water supply shocks, and helps build resilience in climate-sensitive regions like Vayots Dzor, Aragatsotn, and Tavush. Though initial installation costs are higher, drip irrigation reduces long-term costs through lower water bills; reduced fertiliser and pesticide use, and fewer labour inputs.

The invention of modern drip irrigation was developed by Israeli engineer Simcha Blass and the company Netafim in the 1960's, which is now a world leader in irrigation technologies – operating in more than one hundred countries. Drip irrigation has been supported by government subsidies in Israel for farmers to adopt efficient systems, mandatory metering and pricing of all water use, and agricultural extension services to help farmers optimise use. Today, over 75 percent of Israel's irrigated farmland uses drip irrigation resulting up to 60 percent reduction in water use and increasing crop yields.[119] This has enabled Israel to grow more with less, becoming a net food exporter despite severe water scarcity, and thereby creating a thriving agri-tech export sector.

Chapter Eight

Tax Reform

Citizen Based Taxation

Armenia like many international countries utilises a residency-based taxation approach. This means Armenian citizens pay their annual tax returns based on their residency status, rather than citizenship status. An individual is considered a tax resident of Armenia if they spend 183 days or more in Armenia within a calendar year, or have their centre of vital interests (eg. primary economic or personal ties) in Armenia.

As of 2023, Armenia employs a flat income tax rate of 20 percent on wages and salaries for both residents and non-residents. Armenian tax residents can claim a foreign tax credit for taxes paid abroad. This credit is limited to the amount of Armenian tax that would be due on the same income.

Armenia's residency-based taxation means that expatriates are taxed on their worldwide income only if they meet the residency criteria.

One option for the Armenian government to consider, even though it may be politically unpopular, is a taxation system based on citizenship not residency, a system which the United States applies to its citizens. In order to consider the proposal, it should consider a feasibility study, which would seek feedback from stakeholders on how it could apply such a step. The review should also consider economic analysis and modelling on potential revenue, in addition to costs for applying such a system.

This could also apply to Armenian citizens who are temporarily expatriates working in a foreign country, or diaspora Armenian who hold Armenian citizenship. Furthermore, for diaspora Armenians, this additional onus should lead to additional rights.

The US applies taxes to its citizens on worldwide income regardless of where they reside. Even if they live and work abroad full-time and pay local taxes, they still have to file a US tax return each year and potentially pay additional US taxes. Even if no tax is owed, they must still file if their income exceeds certain thresholds. The US has mechanisms to avoid double taxation, such as Foreign Earned Income Exclusion (FEIE), which allows exclusion of a certain amount of foreign-earned income, Foreign Tax Credit (FTC), which gives credit for taxes paid to other countries, and tax treaties and agreements to minimise double taxation.

The potential benefits would be an opportunity to raise additional revenue, and estimates vary based on various modelling. It could also deter tax-motivated emigration and align taxation with national benefits.

The challenges and risks are various, which is a reason it has not been adopted widely across the world. These challenges include: administrative complexity, hard to monitor foreign income and enforce compliance; citizens may renounce their citizenship to avoid tax burdens; and potentially unpopular with diaspora members holding Armenian citizenship. Many people abroad already pay taxes locally and would want to avoid additional taxation or administrative compliance.

Furthermore, in order to make it effective, countries applying such a system would require access to global banking reporting systems, applicable laws allowing them to penalise non-compliant citizens abroad, and diplomatic agreements to enforce tax collection internationally.

Many would argue that the US is an outlier, and its system works largely because of its global financial influence and infrastructure. That said, given Armenia's large diaspora, which is twice the size of Armenians living in Armenia, this could be seen to be a practical way of investing in the country's future. There are many advantages and disadvantages to such an idea, but a feasibility study could provide an objective way to seriously consider the proposal. Armenia should consider every option at its disposal.

Levies and Expatriates

Another option for consideration could be the imposition of levies or charges on expatriate citizens. These levies may serve fiscal, regulatory, or administrative purposes.

Some countries apply this including the US. This measure has in many instances deterred citizens renouncing US citizenship. When US citizens give up their citizenship (and long-term green card holders), they may be subject to a tax on their net worth. If the individual sold all assets on the day before expatriation—capital gains are calculated and taxed. This only applies if their net worth exceeds $2 million or if average annual net income tax for the prior five years exceeds around $190,000. This helps prevent tax avoidance by wealthy individuals renouncing citizenship.[120]

Philippines requires mandatory contributions for overseas Filipino Workers. Another example is Eritrea which imposes a two percent diaspora tax, and applies to Eritrean citizens living abroad. It is a two percent tax on global income of Eritrean expatriates. It is claimed to fund national reconstruction. The tax has faced criticisms.

Singapore does not impose exit taxes or global income taxes. However, it does levy foreign worker levies, not on citizens, but on employers of foreign workers, which indirectly affects expatriate job prospects and salaries.

China applies taxation of global income of its citizens. Residents are subject to individual income tax on their global income. Non-residents are taxed only on income sourced within China. An individual is considered a tax resident if they reside in China for 183 days or more in a calendar year. Continuous residence for six years without a single absence of more than 30 days resets the count, potentially subjecting the individual to taxation on global income.[121]

As mentioned earlier, an individual is considered a tax resident of Armenia if they spend 183 days or more in Armenia within a calendar year, or have their centre of vital interests (eg, primary economic or personal ties) in Armenia. If an individual is not a tax resident, Armenia does not tax their foreign income. Non-residents (including expatriates) must pay tax on income earned from Armenian sources, such as rental income from property in Armenia, dividends or capital gains from Armenian companies, and work physically performed in Armenia (even short-term).

Chapter Nine

The Art of the Deal

The Art of the Deal is a book written by Donald Trump with journalist Tony Schwartz, published in 1987.[122] It is a part memoir, part business advice book that outlines Trump's approach to deal-making, negotiation, and success in business.

The book emphasises the importance of thinking big and taking calculated risks, while advocating for leveraging assets and using debt strategically. Its negotiation tactics include maximising leverage, entering negotiations from a position of strength, knowing the market, understanding demand, trends, and competitors, making bold first offers, and starting with high expectations to leave room for negotiation.

It is somewhat ironic then that US President Donald Trump presided over a trilateral summit between Armenian Prime Minister Nikol Pashinyan, and Azerbaijani President Ilham Aliyev which took place at the White House on 8 August 2025, resulting in a joint declaration for peace.

That declaration detailed the closure of OSCE's Minsk Process, and unimpeded connectivity between Azerbaijan and its Nakhichevan Autonomous region through Armenia – which has been labelled as the 'Trump Route for International Peace and Prosperity' (TRIPP) connectivity project and provides the US exclusive rights on that land for 99 years. The declaration also includes platitudes seeking peace.

Notably, the joint declaration made no mention of Armenian territories currently occupied by Azerbaijani forces along the border, the right of Armenians to return to Artsakh, or the fate of Armenian prisoners currently held in Baku. There was no reference to the ethnic cleansing of Artsakh carried out by Azerbaijan in 2023, the 2020 war launched by Azerbaijan, or the numerous documented war crimes against Armenian civilians and soldiers.

The declaration also omitted any acknowledgment of the destruction of Armenian cultural heritage, the displacement of over 100,000 Armenians from their ancestral lands, or the ongoing persecution of Armenians under Azerbaijani control. Likewise absent was mention of the trials in Baku against the former leaders of Artsakh, as well as the broader pattern of human rights abuses and violations of international law committed by Azerbaijan in recent years.

To top it off, because of the declaration, President Trump waived Section 907 of the Freedom Support Act, removing the US prohibition on military assistance to Azerbaijan.

If someone were to examine the relations between Armenia and Azerbaijan after the Artsakh war in 2020, they would come to the conclusion that Armenia has not leveraged any of these tactics detailed in *The Art of the Deal*; instead this has been implemented by Azerbaijan.

Let's go through these systematically. From the outset, following the Artsakh war, Azerbaijan took bold positions to settle the conflict, including:

- Constitutional Amendments. Azerbaijan has insisted that Armenia revise its constitution to remove any clauses that imply territorial claims over Azerbaijani land.
- Dissolution of the Organisation for Security and Co-operation (OSCE) Minsk Group.
- Border villages. Armenia acceding to Azeri demands to return border villages Baghanis Ayrum, Asagi Eskipara, Heyrimli, Kizilhacili.
- Zangezur Corridor. Proposed transportation route intended to connect mainland Azerbaijan with its exclave, Nakhichevan, by passing through Armenia's Syunik Province (which one could argue is not necessary, given Azerbaijan already uses such a corridor through Iran).
- Goris to Kapan. In November 2021, Azerbaijan established additional border checkpoints on roads between the Armenian cities of Goris and Kapan in Syunik Province, effectively extending its control over these critical routes. This move

disrupted local transportation and forced Armenia to develop another transportation road corridor inland at significant cost.

- Syunik Airport. Armenia's regional airport servicing its southern Syunik province, which is located approximately four kilometres east of Kapan, is situated in close proximity to the Armenia-Azerbaijan border, in some parts less than 100 metres, making it strategically vulnerable.

- EU monitoring. Armenia has agreed to withdraw European Union monitors from the Armenian-Azerbaijani border, once a peace deal is settled.[123] The European Union has a monitoring mission in Armenia along the border of Azerbaijan to monitor any violations of the ceasefire, and its mandate was extended until February 2027.

- Legal disputes. The declaration mentions that *"The conditions have been created for our nations to finally embark on building good neighbourly relations on the basis of the inviolability of international borders and the inadmissibility of the use of force for the acquisition of territory after the conflict that brought immense human suffering."*[124] Azerbaijan has sought to end any future claims from Armenia.

Some would argue that Armenia had no choice, losing a war and two generations of young men who gave the ultimate sacrifice, their life to defend their homeland. A country tired of war, seeking security, peace and stability.

One would sadly be naïve to believe that these demands guarantee security and stability. There are several common sayings and idioms related to giving in to a bully or conceding under pressure: *"Give an inch, they'll take a mile."* – If you give in, even a little, the bully will take advantage and demand even more; and *"Appeasement only emboldens aggression."* – Giving in to demands doesn't stop bullying, it often encourages more.

At every point, rather than providing a counter negotiating position, Armenia has appeared to accede. There are a number of alternatives Armenia could have entertained as part of negotiations leading to the joint declaration. These could have included:

- Constitutional Amendments. Armenia should also seek reciprocally Azerbaijan's constitution has no territorial demands over sovereign Armenia and that it refrain from the use of so-called Western Azerbaijan, which President of Azerbaijan Aliyev consistently uses.[125]

- Zangezur corridor. Counter Azerbaijani demands with Armenia having a similar corridor through Nakhichevan to Iran. This would drastically reduce transportation times for Armenia to Iran, avoiding its mountainous transportation sector – and, furthermore, demand a fee from Azerbaijan for every vehicle using the Zangezur corridor.

- Border villages. The demarcation line between both countries could be consistently disputed with various Soviet era maps, which often changed. If Azerbaijan demanded border villages, Armenia should have demanded Artsvashen which formed part of Soviet Armenia, initially connected to Armenia by a peninsular land corridor, but later became an enclave within Soviet Azerbaijan following another change by Soviet authorities. There are other border villages based on various versions of Soviet era maps.

- Goris to Kapan. Armenia incurred a significant financial cost in having to build a new road linking Goris to Kapan and should have demanded financial compensation from Azerbaijan as part of negotiating this demand.

- Syunik Airport. It is unclear, what if any steps were taken to create a demarcation line at least a few kilometres from the airport, rather than in some place 100 metres away, making it a strategic threat. There could have been more steps to create a 'demilitarised zone' within a few kilometres around this strategic infrastructure.

- EU monitoring. Azerbaijan has no authority if Armenia chooses to have third party monitors on its borders. Armenia is a sovereign country and can choose which mechanism are to its benefit, especially given the high level of threats from Azerbaijan.

- Territorial occupation. Azerbaijan maintains military forces on internationally recognised Armenian territory, following its September 2023 offensive and previous conflicts, which is estimated at 215 square kilometres. Despite international calls to withdraw, it hasn't. A simple non-starter for negotiations for Armenia.

- Legal disputes. Armenia could have withheld any commitments to future legal claims through international courts or otherwise regarding Azerbaijan's invasion and subsequent actions, which could be legitimately challenged.

The last point is very important. During the 30 years when Artsakh was an Armenian controlled territory, at no point did Azerbaijan withhold its claims over the territory. Conversely, Armenia has not effectively leveraged its right to withhold future claims.

Every country has at its disposal a position to negotiate. In order to do so, they need to fully understand the levers at their disposal and be willing to seek a counter claim.

A key concern remains Azerbaijan's illegal detainment of Armenian political prisoners, most notably Armenian leaders in the Artsakh government. The Armenian government has been relatively quiet in any demands made public. Some may argue through diplomatic channels, behind public scrutiny can be more effective.

The Ministry of Foreign Affairs of Armenia has condemned the detentions, labelling them as violations of international humanitarian law, and despite raising the issue with international bodies, including the International Court of Justice, it has at the same time signalled withdrawing these claims in the pursuit of a peace agreement.[126]

Internationally, entities such as the European Parliament have called for the immediate release of the Armenian detainees, highlighting the broader geopolitical implications and human rights concerns associated with their continued imprisonment. The joint declaration for peace between Armenia and Azerbaijan makes no reference to these political prisoners, which means Azerbaijan will continue to use this as a bargaining chip for other concessions, in other words, using tactics outlined in *The Art of the Deal.*

So, what should the Armenian government do? It can do many things. It can start by taking a clear public stance and officially demand the release of the prisoners. Silence or ambiguity can be seen as tacit acceptance or weakness. It can reinforce solidarity with the affected families by regularly engaging them, intensify efforts through the International Court of Justice (ICJ) and European Court of Human Rights (ECHR) to argue violations of the Geneva Conventions and international humanitarian law, provide consistent updates on the status of the prisoners and diplomatic efforts. Lack of communication breeds frustration and misinformation. There can be Armenian government observers at the trials in Azerbaijan. Many of these points have been raised by Jared Gensen, international human rights lawyer for Ruben Vardanyan.[127]

The Armenian government should appoint a Special Envoy to lead the negotiation for their release, and act as the main contact for the families seeking information, as well as the Armenian public. This is a recommendation also made by Jared Gensen and carries common sense. Special Envoys are diplomatic tools used widely in the international community and diplomatic circles including the United States for addressing specific geographical areas or policy issues. This Envoy could be a serving or former Ambassador, or private citizen.

When it comes to negotiating, Armenia often negotiates from a position of constraint, due to geography, security challenges, and economic limitations. Armenia is seen as a principled but geopolitically vulnerable actor.

The Art of the Deal demonstrates that Armenia has not leveraged its negotiating position at all. Seeking peace is a noble goal, but it is something that is negotiated and reciprocated, it should not come at any price.

Chapter Ten

The Diaspora Reimagined

In the first edition of Smart Nation, there was an examination on the importance of the diaspora as a vital resource for Armenia, how diasporan organisations could be structured, and specific diasporan communities. This chapter will focus on specifically diasporan rights in Armenia, should they become citizens, and explore other large diasporan communities globally to see how they leverage with references to Israel, India, and Greece.

It is estimated that there are about ten million Armenians around the globe, with seven million residing in the diaspora. Although there is no explicit separate status under Armenian law for dual citizens, they are theoretically equal in civil, economic, and social rights. There remain some gaps which could be addressed.

Armenian citizens cannot vote in parliamentary or local elections unless they are physically present in Armenia. They also cannot be elected to most public offices without fulfilling a minimum continuous residency requirement (usually four to six years). Diaspora Armenians who acquire citizenship before the age of 27 may become liable for conscription unless they pay a government-approved exemption fee or reside abroad and are exempted based on bilateral agreements (eg, in Russia, France).

For a comparative overview, Israel is the most open when it applies diaspora citizenship rights. Unlike Armenia, they offer absentee voting in elections and dual citizens can attain high office. They also provide full consular support for dual citizens. India, by comparison, is the most restrictive with dual citizenship, voting from overseas, eligibility for high office are all restricted.

If there is appetite for reform for Armenia regarding diaspora citizenship rights, a number of areas could be considered, such as enabling voting abroad for diaspora citizens (via embassies or digital ballots), loosen office restrictions for dual nationals with long-standing engagement, enhance consular protection frameworks for dual nationals.

Preservation of Western Armenian

Western Armenian is becoming endangered, and in some dialects, nearly extinct. It is both a linguistic crisis and a cultural emergency. It reflects the lasting trauma of the Armenian Genocide, the dispersal of Western Armenians into the diaspora. In 2010, UNESCO classified Western Armenian as a 'definitely endangered language.' This declaration immediately raised awareness of its impending extinction.

The Armenian government's 2021–26 national strategy proposed giving Western Armenian a 'special status' within Armenia. Calouste Gulbenkian Foundation, in partnership with Armenian government bodies, supports the Armenian Communities Department in publishing, media, digitisation, and app development focused on Western Armenian.

Armenia's Ministry of Education, Science, Culture and Sports approved a national Strategy on Preservation, Development, and Popularisation of Culture, supporting Western Armenian curricula and literature publishing. Western Armenian shouldn't just be characterised as a language spoken in the diaspora. Armenia has seen recent waves of Armenian migration from Syria and Lebanon, notably during the Syrian conflict and the rise of ISIS when it governed parts of Syria and Iraq. An estimated migration of more than 50,000.

Western Armenian has a historical legacy in Soviet Armenia. Gyumri, Armenia's second largest city hosted large numbers of Armenian refugees fleeing the Ottoman empire from the Armenian Genocide in 1915. Many of these people spoke the Karin (Garin) dialect of Armenian but, over time, Eastern Armenian and Russian words have been incorporated into the dialect.

There was also a wave of Armenians coming from the Middle East who were Western Armenian speaking as part of repatriation efforts in the late 1940's and early 1950's. They moved to Soviet

Figure 8. Comparative Overview: Diaspora Citizenship Rights

	Armenia	Israel	Greece	India
Dual citizenship	✔	✔	✔	✘
Diaspora path to citizenship	✔	✔	✔	⚠
Right to vote abroad	✘	✔	✔	✘
Eligibility for high office	⚠	✔	✔	✘
Military obligations	⚠	✔	⚠	✘
Property rights	✔	✔	✔	✔
Taxation	⚠	✔	✔	✔
Consular protection for dual nationality	⚠	✔	✔	✘

✔ Allowed/required   ⚠ Limitations/conditions   ✘ Not allowed

Armenia and many use the Eastern Armenian dialect spoken in Armenia.

In Armenia, Western Armenian language media does exist, but it remains limited in scope and reach. Several initiatives, both state-supported and civil society-driven, have emerged in recent years to revive and support Western Armenian, especially for the benefit of diasporan communities and repatriates.

There are some steps that can be taken to further preserve Western Armenian, including, establishing a weekly Western Armenian news and culture program on Public Television of Armenia, H1; Western Armenian as an elective module in public schools where diaspora children are enrolled, and implementing a national awareness campaign, 'Two Branches, One Language,' to educate the Armenian public on the value of Western Armenian.

Diaspora-Armenia Relations

The diaspora is estimated to be seven million Armenians globally and is a resource that can significantly benefit Armenian statehood. There continues to be misunderstanding from both perspectives. The diaspora image of Armenia can vary based on personal experience and not always connected to reality, or genuine difficulties Armenians in Armenia face.

Armenia also misjudges the diaspora, viewing them as a conglomerate, without fully understanding its intricacies nor how to leverage properly. This results in misconceptions and a resource not fully leveraged until this day.

According to the World Bank, the size of the Armenian economy in terms of GDP in 2024 was $25.8 billion.[128] In per capita terms around $8,500 per person. In 2016, when the first edition of Smart Nation was published, the economy was estimated at around $10 billion. During that period, there has been around 150 percent growth, a strengthening of the national currency dram, and significant rise in costs.

Armenia is today considered a developing, upper-middle-income economy with strong growth but significant challenges ahead before achieving 'developed' status.

Any approach to Armenia needs to be seen through this lense. And despite the well meaning efforts of many Armenian diasporan organisations in fundraising efforts for many worthy projects, what is needed is national building projects to help propel the Armenian economy to the next level.

For context, during the 2020 Artsakh war, the diaspora mobilised and it was estimated more than $200 million was raised through the All-Armenia Fund. In addition, organisations like the Armenian General Benevolent Union (AGBU) raised millions for humanitarian aid, the Armenian Relief Society provided medical supplies and social services, raising several million dollars; churches, local charities, and private initiatives also contributed. If we combine these amounts, it could be estimated that more than $250 million was raised, the largest amount ever in the history of the diaspora. That goodwill was tested when there were questions raised about the transparency of how the All-Armenia Funds were being managed and spent.[129] The Armenian government took over direct management of a sizable part of the funds, promising to apply it toward humanitarian purposes. What was an opportunity bringing together the diaspora in times of a crises, became diluted due to controversy.

Furthermore, although the funds raised were critical for immediate humanitarian needs, for comparison purposes, all the funds that were raised in this record effort were equivalent to only one Patriot (PAC-3 Battery), long range air defence system.

Also, why did the diaspora need to wait for a crisis to mobilise? The current predicament of Armenia requires constant alert and vigilance. In other words, this effort, while noteworthy and significant, should occur every year with the view of nation building efforts and needs to be done in a climate of trust, transparency, and clear accountability.

Further complicating Diaspora-Armenia relations is the absence of a single unifying umbrella organization to represent the many diverse groups that exist. That limits the impact the diaspora can have compared to a united and combined voice. In Armenia, political differences can be managed through the local political process, in the diaspora, rather than politics, what should be the focus is nation building efforts, in addition to helping support local communities.

The Armenian government's main vehicle for managing diaspora relations is through the Office of the High Commissioner for Diaspora Affairs. The Armenian government has undertaken several initiatives to help diaspora relations. These include Come Home – 'Ari Tun,' a two-week immersive summer experience for teenagers, Diaspora Youth Ambassador Program for young adults to network and represent Armenia globally, iGorts Fellowship Program, bringing together diaspora professionals into government roles for around one year; a Repatriation and Integration Centre to streamline repatriation for newcomers, DiasPro Volunteer Professionals Program to match diaspora experts with Armenian institutions for voluntary contributions, NerUzh, which supports diaspora-led tech startups considering relocation or expansion to Armenia, and other initiatives.

In addition, non government organisations like Birthright Armenia and Repat Armenia have youth volunteering and cultural immersion experiences, supporting repatriation and long-term integration for diasporan Armenian relocating to Armenia. All these steps together are meaningful and provide much more opportunities for Armenian youth and repatriates seeking a deeper connection with Armenia.

However, the leadership of the Armenian government has on several occasions taken missteps when dealing with the diaspora, which it should treat as a partner, rather than a subject.

In 2025, Prime Minister Pashinyan, while meeting with leaders of the Swiss Armenian community, suggested the need to 'revisit' the history of the Armenian Genocide, questioning the timing and motivations behind its international recognition. *"We must also revisit the history of the Armenian genocide… How is it that in 1939 there was no Armenian genocide [recognition] agenda, and how is it that in 1950 the Armenian genocide agenda emerged?"*[130]

This comment is reflective of many things. First, the trauma of diasporan Armenians who survived genocide. Their focus was survival, and when that is your focus, that is where your energy is diverted. It took another generation to begin with recognition efforts in numerous ways. This psychology of the diaspora needs to be understood.

In June 2025, Prime Minister Pashinyan described Artsakh as a 'noose' that prevented Armenia's development. *"There is a lot of talk that we have lost Nagorno-Karabagh. I have thought a lot about this issue and concluded that we have not lost Nagorno-Karabagh, but have found the Republic of Armenia."*[131] During a rally in Artsakh's capital, Stepanakert in August 2019, the Prime Minister emphatically declared: "Artsakh is Armenia, and that's it!"[132] This deliberate mixed signalling not only within Armenia but to diasporan communities is a gross loss in trust. Not only words used, but perceived hypocrisy which is very difficult to recover from.

In June 2025, the Armenian government arrested clerics, part of the Armenian Apostolic Church, accusing them of being part of a criminal oligarchy and plotting a coup. This has led to a feud involving the Catholicos of All Armenians and the Prime Minister. Not only does the church have spiritual influence of a country that first adopted Christianity as its official religion in 301AD, it has an influential role in diasporan communities across the globe.

Prime Minister Pashinyan, very short succession, has inflamed diasporan relations by his approach to sacred issues involving the Armenian genocide, Artsakh, and the Armenian Apostolic Church.

Let's for a moment assume these issues can be overcome. What can and should the Armenian government do to deepen meaningful diaspora ties to strengthen statehood?

In June 2025, NVIDIA and AI-cloud developer Firebird announced launching a $500 million AI supercomputer (AI Factory) in Armenia, scheduled to be operational by 2026. This is Armenia's most ambitious technology investment, ushering in cutting-edge AI cloud services. There were a number of diasporan Armenians involved to make this announcement a reality working alongside the Armenian government. This included Rev. Lebaredian, Vice President, NVIDIA; Razmig Hovaghimian, Co-founder and CEO of Firebird AI; Noubar Afeyan, The Afeyan Foundation, an investor in Firebird AI; as well as local Armenian Alexander Yesayan Co-founder and Chair Team Telecom Armenia.

In March 2025, Starlink officially began offering satellite internet services in Armenia, making it the 130th country to receive the service. Razmig Hovaghimian was again involved playing a key liaison with Armenian officials, helping bridge communication between SpaceX and Armenia's tech community. This is a transformational project providing speeds up to 220 Mbps, available in rural villages, mountains, and underserved areas, and supporting digital inclusion efforts by helping remote education, telemedicine, and communication during emergencies.

There are of course many other examples, but the point here is that the diaspora and Armenia need to work closer together to make meaningful transformational projects in Armenia which directly impacts the country's trajectory. A critical area in this regard is national and cyber security.

Other than waiting for an Armenian in the diaspora who is in an influential position to initiate such a change, how can the Armenian government proactively leverage these highly connected, influential and impactful Armenians? Eric Hagopian from Civilnet suggested the first thing it can do is to ask for help. It may sound simple but this is not a given. Hagopian also stressed that the diaspora is needed to contribute towards nation building projects.[133] Indeed, the Government could produce a list of nation building significant projects where there is a skills gap or shortage and offer the opportunity for diasporan Armenians to participate on a project basis or otherwise. This must be seen as a natural progression to initiatives like iGorts or other such initiatives. These are targeted high value impactful projects that influence the country's future.

An example where this works effectively is the way the Indian government works with ethnic Indian CEOs and senior executives of leading multinational companies. In the technology sector alone, Companies like Microsoft, Alphabet, IBM, Adobe, and Palo Alto Networks all have CEO's that are of Indian heritage. Many others would have senior leaders or members of the company's leadership teams.

India has used its geostrategic position as a counter weight to China, in addition to having a significant talent pool to attract technology investment in its country. Outside of the US, India has become one of the sizeable international markets for these companies for employment, and provision of skilled services. For example, Microsoft has more than 20,000 employees across 10 Indian cities.[134]

The Indian government engages proactively and strategically with global tech CEOs of Indian heritage—not just for diaspora diplomacy, but as part of a nation-building and tech diplomacy agenda. These engagements are designed to attract investment, secure partnerships, enhance India's digital reputation, and foster innovation ecosystems.

Prime Minister Modi and key cabinet ministers regularly meet global Indian-origin CEOs during official visits, summits, or bilateral dialogues. Invest India and MeitY (Ministry of Electronics & IT) maintain channels with diaspora CEOs for investment facilitation and policy input. Pravasi Bharatiya Divas (PBD) is the flagship diaspora engagement summit, where Indian-origin CEOs are honoured and consulted. Prime Minister Modi personally invited Indian-origin tech leaders to advise on India's semiconductor mission and AI taskforce.

There are many Armenians either in senior leadership positions or have direct access to CEO's of those and other organisations. Not to mention many other prolific Armenian entrepreneurs who have their own significant networks in the tech sector such as Alexis Ohanian, Magdalena Yesil, co-founders of ServiceTitan, Ara Mahdessian & Vahe, and so many others. These talents need to be engaged strategically.

Another area which the Armenian diaspora could be more effectively engaged is in diplomacy. Armenians from across the globe have served as Ambassadors for their respective countries, Ministers, heads of Departments, Governors, Premiers and many other positions, all of whom carry expertise in diplomacy or the inner workings of government. Even their local connections within the governments they represented or worked for is not actively cultivated or leveraged. They could be deployed in a wide array of scenarios for Armenia, whether it be a Special Envoy for delicate negotiations, help resolve internal challenges in Departments that they may have experienced before, helping with influential connections within government (not just those with titles but those that carry influence in decision making). In order to do this, the Armenian government must actively identify and seek their assistance. It is too often the case the government may see this as a compromise on their sovereignty, control, or reluctance to share information.

Diaspora-Armenia relations is a two-way process, it needs to be underpinned by trust, mutual respect, and a common shared vision. This requires real leadership on both sides.

Chapter Eleven

Trust in Government

Trust in any government is fundamental for legitimacy and social cohesion, effective policy implementation, civic engagement, economic stability, and responding to crises. Successive Armenian governments have had problems in trust with its population. Whether it be matters relating to corruption, oligarchies, embezzlement, or abuse of power.

Trust is the highest single value and commodity a government can have with its population. Trust takes a long time to earn and can be lost very quickly. It requires constant work and effort. The Artsakh war in 2020 also fundamentally impacted trust. The Armenian public was provided information that did not correspond to what was occurring on the ground. Armenia gave the impression it could defend itself, but it found that it had lost a war, and also the trust of its population. How did we get here?

Historical Landscape

Following Armenia's independence in 1991 from the Soviet Union, the country faced a serious economic crisis followed by a war in Nagorno-Karabagh. The country's first President in the Modern Republic was Levon Ter-Petrosyan, a leader in the Nagorno-Karabagh movement. This was also a very difficult time for the country and economy facing conflict and trying to rebuild the economy following the collapse of the Soviet Union.

In 1998, Levon Ter-Petrosyan, resigned due to disagreements with the country's other leaders regarding the Armenian strategy for resolving the Nagorno-Karabagh conflict. Taking over as the country's President was Robert Kocharyan, who had previously served as Prime Minister (1992 to 1994) and President (1994 to 1997) of Nagorno-Karabagh.

A terrorist attack on October 27, 1999 fatally impacted the key leaders of the country, including Prime Minister Vazgen Sargsyan and

Speaker of Parliament Karen Demirchyan, as well as a number of deputies in the Parliament. Many believe that this event altered the country's course of development, and conspiracies still surround how this occurred and why – further undermining trust.

During Robert Kocharyan's Presidency, the country experienced economic growth and deepening ties with Russia. Kocharyan was also accused of accumulating significant personal wealth by illegitimate means. He also imposed a crackdown on post-election protests in 2008.

In 2008, Serzh Sargsyan was elected President, replacing Robert Kocharyan and defeating former President Levon Ter-Petrosyan. A government crackdown on protests resulted in the deaths of ten individuals. At the time, Nikol Pashinyan, who was involved with the opposition, was accused of organising mass disorders and inciting violence, thus becoming a fugitive.

In 2015, constitutional changes stipulated a transition from a semi-presidential to a parliamentary form of government. This was seen as an attempt by the ruling party and its then leader Serzh Sargsyan to consolidate power and maintain its grip on the government.

The constitutional amendments provided an opportunity for a single party to control both the executive and judiciary through a one-party legislature. Sargsyan's transition to the Prime Minister's office, following the completion of his second Presidential term in April 2018, proved to be unsuccessful. The Velvet Revolution, then led by former journalist and parliamentary opposition member Nikol Pashinyan, galvanised popular protests and managed to oust the government. This change led to new expectations from the Armenian government, including addressing corruption and many other issues that impacted on trust.

In 2020 and 2023, with the loss of the war on Artsakh, the public's trust was tested again given the information it was provided on the war and the unforeseen defeat. It was uncovered that some military officers had embezzled funds intended for weapons and supplies.[135] Prime Minister Pashinyan came under intense criticism for the defeat. His position in relation to Artsakh, saying it is part of Armenia on one hand, and then conceding it after defeat to Azerbaijan has further eroded public trust.

Armenia is categorised as a defective democracy.[136] Challenges remain in judicial independence, media freedom, and political polarisation.

The Caucasus Barometer survey in 2024 found distrust in political parties, sitting at 51 percent in 2024.[137] The parliament and the executive government (Prime Minister and Cabinet Ministers) are considered as the entities most distrusted by the public with full distrust 50 percent and 42 percent, respectively. Levels of trust in the President have remained relatively consistent within the three years.

In 2024, the International Republican Institute found Prime Minister Nikol Pashinyan trust rating stood at a poor 16 percent.[138] The results reflect a steep decline in public faith in politicians since 2018. The Armenian government's inability to meet initial expectations for rapid reform, combined with Armenia's decisive defeat in the second Artsakh War, have acted as the main catalysts for changing attitudes. This declining trend needs to be addressed.

International Comparisons

According to the *World Population Review,*[139] small states populate the highest trust in government. It is led by Switzerland, followed by Luxembourg, Finland, Sweden, and Norway.

High levels of trust in government tends to stem from a combination of transparent governance, strong institutions, social cohesion, and service delivery.

Finland has transparent institutions, consistently ranked top by Transparency International. It has low corruption with strong mechanisms for accountability, and effective public services such as high-quality education, health, and welfare. Its civic engagement allows citizens to have real influence over policymaking. Its cultural values provide a strong norm of honesty and consensus politics.

In Singapore, government remains the most trusted institution, even exceeding non-profit organisations, business, and media.[140] The reasons include competent, technocratic governance with an efficient and effective public administration that runs the country like a large, well-functioning company. There is low corruption with strong rule of law and enforcement. Public officials are paid handsomely, reducing the risk of corruption. The government delivers strong growth and public services, and despite limited political pluralism, the public accept it from results-driven legitimacy.

Although this book is not advocating for Armenia to be less plural, there are many lessons to be learnt that adopt practices to help with increased level of trust in government. Armenia should seek to actively cultivate and learn from other small nation states who have consistently delivered strong levels of trust in government.

Real Armenia Doctrine Should Be One Armenia

In 2025, Prime Minister Pashinyan advocated a controversial interpretation of Armenian history, which could have a direct bearing on levels of trust with government. The "Real Armenia" doctrine, which he advocated, seeks to define the Republic of Armenia in its currently internationally recognised borders of 29,743 square kilometres.[141]

The motivation for this doctrine seeks to modernise the Armenian constitution, to remove any clauses that imply territorial claims over Azerbaijan, which Azerbaijan has demanded in exchange for peace with Armenia, despite Azerbaijan's constitution having similar claims over Armenia.

Prime Minister Pashinyan sparked controversy by questioning the political utility of Mount Ararat, an iconic national symbol, which is located in present day Turkey, given it is represented in Armenia's national emblem – particularly in state symbols like the Armenian coat of arms.[142] He argued that using a mountain not within Armenia's current borders sends conflicting messages and could be seen as undermining Armenia's internationally recognised territorial integrity. This type of thinking represents the "Real Armenia" doctrine.

Mount Ararat is more than a geographical landmark, it's deeply embedded in Armenian culture, history, religion, and diaspora consciousness. Removing or diminishing it is seen as undermining Armenian identity. Pashinyan's remarks reflect his broader strategy of seeking to revise the concept of Armenian identity, emphasising present-day realities over historical claims, to support his conciliatory foreign policy toward Turkey and Azerbaijan.

In 2024, Prime Minister Pashinyan posted an innocuous seeming photo on his Instagram page, a snowy mountain with the caption 'Aragats. The highest peak of the Republic of Armenia, 4,090 meters.' Though this is factually correct as defined by Armenia's current borders, Mount Ararat is in fact taller than Aragats by more than 1,000 metres and imposes itself, clearly seen from Yerevan and various parts of Armenia. Then to top it off in September 2025, Prime Minister Pashinyan announced the government would remove the image of Mount Ararat from the entry and exit passport stamps of Armenia effective from November 2025.

Enunciating the "Real Armenia" doctrine, Pashinyan had previously said, *"Should the real Armenia serve the historical Armenia or should the historical Armenia serve the real Armenia?"*[143]

In order for a historical Armenia to serve the real Armenia, it needs to be properly recognised, respected, and treated with pride. Armenia's boundaries have consistently changed through previous Armenian Kingdoms, the 1918 Republic of Armenia, Soviet Armenia, Armenian independence in 1991, and again following the Artsakh war in 2020 and 2023. It is neither static nor set in stone.

The representation of the Republic of Armenia does not stop at its current border, because those borders have consistently changed, and Armenians are indigenous peoples to their lands going back millennia. To define Armenia within current borders on a map is overly simplistic.

That said, no one denies that the focus on economic, infrastructure, health, education, defence should all relate to existing borders, but applying a "Real Armenia" doctrine is not a unifying concept. It could be applied to modern nation states which do not carry historical legacies or are not inhabited by indigenous people, but Armenia is not one of those states and is surrounded by hostile neighbours who have succeeded in many instances to erase Armenian populations.

The '"Real Armenia" doctrine misreads the balance between strategic adaptation and symbolic continuity. By discarding key pillars of Armenian identity and relying on unreciprocated symbolic concessions, it undermines both internal legitimacy and external deterrence.

A more effective strategy would involve embracing symbolic heritage as part of soft power, pursuing a 360 degree foreign policy, but from a position of dignity and narrative strength, building state capacity without denying cultural memory.

A more appropriate doctrine would be a "One Armenia" approach. A "One Armenia" doctrine would provide unity among Armenians within Armenia and around the globe. It would seek to define Armenia not within current borders but would embrace its broader heritage. It would send a clear message that when it comes to the interest of Armenia, Armenians are unified.

Such a doctrine could affirm the sovereignty of the Republic of Armenia within its borders—but without abandoning the memory, culture, or symbols of historical parts of Armenia. The concept of the Armenian nation does not end at its borders. It extends into every Armenian around the world.

Chapter Twelve

Human Capital

This book is called Smart Nation to reflect Armenia's most prized asset, its people and human capital.

Human capital refers to the knowledge, skills, competencies, creativity of a nation's people. Unlike natural resources or physical infrastructure, human capital is a renewable resource that grows with education, training, and experience.

Many small states often have to rely on their people's innovation, ingenuity and creativity to grow, prosper and succeed, and sustain long-term competitiveness. It is a strategic national resource.

As covered in the first edition of Smart Nation, Armenians around the world have a history of being innovative. They are credited with some well renowned inventions that are used around the globe today. These include positron emission tomography (PET), the first functional brain imaging technology (Michel Poghossian); first magnetic resonance (MR) scanning machine (Raymond Vahan Damadian); automated teller machine (ATM) (Luther George Simjian); truck mounted revolving concrete drum mixer, revolutionising the concrete industry (Stephan Stepanian); first licensed vaccine against rotavirus (Albert Kapikian); pioneer of plastic surgery (Varazdat Kazanjian); pressured inhaler used for asthma, allergies, nasal sprays, eye drops (Roger Altounian); the Soviet MiG military aircraft (Artem Ivanovich Mikoyan); automatic transmission for automobiles (Asadour Sarafian); and many others.

The World Bank's Human Capital Index (HCI) is an international metric that measures human capital and quantifies how much a country is investing in its future workforce and ranges from 0 to 1, with 1 representing the benchmark of full health and complete education.

According to the 2020 HCI Index,[144] Armenia scores 0.58, which places it in the middle tier globally, while small nation states like Singapore are 1st (0.88), Finland 6th (0.80), Ireland 9th (0.79), Estonia 12th (0.78), Slovenia and Norway 14th (0.77), and Israel 28th (0.73).

One area that Singapore excels is grooming public sector leadership and future political leaders. The government offers Public Service Commission (PSC) Scholarships, covering prestigious overseas or local university education in exchange for a bond to serve in the public sector. The administrative service provides accelerated promotions and exposure to senior responsibilities early on, and outstanding civil servants are encouraged to transition into politics, ensuring a pipeline of ministers who already understand governance deeply. This creates continuity between technocratic expertise and political leadership. Singapore has managed to institutionalise government leadership into a system, rather than relying on individuals or ad hoc programs. This pipeline ensures the state always has a bench of well-prepared, highly competent leaders ready to step into critical roles.

It is also a clear and deliberate example of investing in human capital.

In Israel, the government has played a crucial role in using public funds to create a network of venture capital funds, effectively de-risking investments for private foreign capital and providing a spark for the local venture capital ecosystem. Israel has one of the highest number of startups per capita globally and ranked 1st in terms of technology unicorns per capita. A unicorn is when a startup has a valuation at or above $1 billion. As of 2025, the country's startup scene contained 90 active tech unicorns, raising billions of dollars in investments annually.[145]

Finland's education system is world renowned, based around its school system. Public education from preschool to university is free, ensuring equal opportunity for all. The system empowers teachers, who are required to have a master's degree and are given a high degree of autonomy in their classrooms. This allows for a focus on individual student needs and creative teaching methods. This system unleashes creativity at a young age which can have a significant impact later in life, allowing children to think for themselves and learn how to learn. A natural way of upskilling.

Ireland demonstrates excellence in human capital investment by adopting a strategic, industry-aligned education model driven by FDI. It makes talent its primary asset by continuously overhauling its education and training systems. Key government initiatives, such as the Human Capital Initiative and Springboard+, directly fund university and graduate courses in high-demand fields like information technology, data analytics, and AI. These programs, often free or heavily subsidised, rapidly upskill and reskill the population, ensuring a competitive, highly educated workforce that has the highest rate of tertiary education completion in the EU. This agile approach, which features strong collaboration between academic institutions and global companies, makes Ireland's human capital a key attractor for multinational investment. Other initiatives include its National Training Fund, a dedicated fund established by legislation through the National Training Fund Act, to support upskilling and reskilling in employment, training for those seeking employment, and funding for research into the economy's future skills needs. It is primarily resourced through a levy on employers and aims to boost the country's workforce development. This cohesive, long-term national strategy transforms human capital into a sustainable competitive advantage.

While Armenia enjoys one of the highest literacy rates in the globe, there is a recognised need to improve the quality and relevance of education to meet the demands of the modern workforce. As covered in Chapter One, Tumo has played a crucial role in helping provide young people in Armenia the digital skills required for the modern workforce. A successful initiative which has been adopted in many global cities. Once these young people acquire the skills, it is also important to retain them and have jobs for them in the country. For this reason, Armenia needs to position itself as a regional hub for digital talent.

Armenia should market its human capital as a national brand, small in size, but large in capability.

Thereby becoming the Smart Nation not by name, but in reality.

Conclusion

Armenia as a Smart Nation needs to make its vision into a reality.

The journey toward transforming Armenia into a Smart Nation is not an ideal, it is a pressing national imperative. This second edition has highlighted how Armenia can position itself as an influential player in the AI race. It has also exposed the hard truths: Armenia faces systemic vulnerabilities, national security pressures, a foreign policy that needs rebalancing, and a defensive posture that can withstand outside threats.

Other small states whether it be Israel, Singapore, the UAE have demonstrated that size is not a barrier when vision, execution, and trust align. Armenia, too, can define its global relevance not by its geography or past alone, but by its capacity to lead.

Armenia needs to have reassert some pride onto the global stage and take proactive steps to do so. The formation of the S20, an idea proposed by former President Sarkissian is an initiative that Armenia should champion and lead.

For a small country, Armenia does have enviable resources to draw upon whether it be its people, capacity for innovation, water, energy as well as natural resources. These need to be strategically leveraged.

Underpinning all this is there must be a climate of trust between Armenia's key institutions and its people. It must work towards uniting our competitive edge. Policies such as the 'Real Armenia' doctrine, or conflict between church and State, do not help in this regard.

Armenia has what it takes to succeed, prosper and be a Smart Nation.

Armenians, wherever they live—guided by common purpose and unity, can achieve remarkable things.

Acknowledgements

When I first wrote Smart Nation in 2016, I didn't conceive another edition, but I felt a second edition was warranted given what has occurred in Armenia and Artsakh, and what could and should occur.

I thank Ara Safarian from the Gomidas Institute for his unwavering support and role in bringing to life Armenian voices from around the globe. The Gomidas Institute is an institution which must be treasured.

Thank you to Ambassador Edward Djerejian, Stepan Kerkyasharian and Ian Bremmer for lending their voices to the book, and the credibility they bring with it being experts in their domain.

I extend my thanks to Shant Safarian and Sonia Bedrossian for the cover design, also producing the design in the first edition.

I thank family members, friends, supporters, and government officials who have encouraged me and provided their feedback over the years.

Finally, I acknowledge the memory of those men and women who made the ultimate sacrifice for Artsakh, their families, and those who are imprisoned.

Their sacrifice motivates us.

Smart Nation – First Edition Recommendations and Predictions

Recommendation	Result	Notes
1. Armenia will develop its first $1 billion startup	Adopted	Picsart
2. Establish an Innovation and Technology Council	Not adopted	
3. Create an Innovation district in Yerevan	Adopted	'Engineering City' was established in 2018 and is a cutting-edge high-tech hub located in the Nor Nork district of Yerevan. Involving government, the World Bank, and private sector.
4. Adoption of e-Government	Adopted	Armenia has climbed from 87th in 2016 to 48th in 2024 in the UN e-Government Development Index
5. Teach coding in schools	Adopted	
6. Appoint a Special Envoy to address Armenia-Turkey relations	Adopted	Armenia appointed Ruben Rubinyan, Deputy Speaker of the National Assembly, as special envoy in December 2021.
7. Deliver a commissioned report into the economic benefits of open borders between Armenia and Turkey	Adopted	Berlin Economics 2022

8. Special visa free zone within certain identified areas along Armenia-Turkey border	Not adopted	
9. Establish a bilateral agreement for road transportation modelled on the flight agreement between Armenia and Turkey	Not adopted	
10. Share best practices on emergency responses to natural disasters and undertake joint exercises with Turkey	Not adopted	Post the 2023 earthquake in Turkey, Armenian search and rescue teams were deployed to affected areas, and border was temporarily reopened for this purpose.
11. Combine Armenia's Foreign Affairs portfolio with Trade	Not adopted	
12. Extend free economic zones along key borders Iran, Georgia, and Turkey – should borders open.	Adopted in part	Meghri Free Economic zone established in 2017
13. Appoint a minister for women	Not adopted	
14. Comprehensive laws and mechanisms against domestic violence	Adopted in part	In 2017, Armenia passed its initial standalone domestic violence law, with amendments in 2024
15. World Happiness Report – top 50 by 2020, and top 20 by 2030	Adopted in part	Armenia improved from previous ranking of 121st to 87th

16. Establish exchange programs internationally in chess with schools, and share best practices	Adopted	
17. Establish a pecuniary interest register that is publicly available should be a requirement for all Armenian government officials	Adopted	Armenia has a system for declarations of interest and assets for public officials, managed by the Corruption Prevention Commission
18. Publish external meetings (that are not national security sensitive) of the President of Armenia and Ministers	Adopted in part	The Office of the President maintains a section explicitly listing foreign visits and working trips
19. Special courts formed for prosecution of alleged corruption	Adopted	Anti-Corruption Court established in April 2021
20. Compliance training conducted formally with all public officials	Adopted in part	Armenia has adopted the Model Code of Conduct for Public Servants—developed in partnership with the Council of Europe and the Corruption Prevention Commission
21. Report monopolistic behaviour anonymously	Adopted	Government has set up of a digital platform to report corruption anonymously

22. Improved funding for public broadcaster to increase transparency and balance in the media and support investigative journalism	Adopted in part	Although the Armenian government funds Public Television of Armenia, independent investigative journalism lacks formal support
23. Implement a digital identity system to provide the full complement of digital government services	Adopted	Implemented digital identity Yesem 'It's me' in 2023
24. Establish a Presidential advisory board to deal with cost-of-living issues	Not adopted	The government is trying to address cost of living issues without a formal board
25. Gradual introduction to electronic voting as a complimentary alternative to current voting methods	Adopted in part	Only a limited number of voters gave been eligible
26. Undertake additional steps to reduce voter fraud	Adopted	An Electoral Code has been adopted and updated to reduce manipulation. Voter identification methods have improved, more cameras and monitoring at polling stations, and fraud hotline established
27. Improve consultation process and increase transparency through Community Cabinets	Not adopted	

28. Develop and implement regional tourism plan, to encourage tourism in Armenia's regions beyond capital	Adopted	Tourism and Regional Infrastructure Project
29. Diaspora - Establishment of national councils representing all community groups within a country	Not adopted	
30. Be a leader in soft power	Not adopted	
31. Nagorno–Karabagh, move from conflict management to conflict resolution	Adopted in part	A joint declaration for peace has been signed, but Armenia extracted no concessions and conceded many points to Azerbaijan

Smart Nation – Second Edition Recommendations and Predictions

Recommendation/Predictions
1. Armenia will develop its first home grown $10 billion startup
2. Implement AI specific initiatives i) Develop a National AI Plan ii) Appoint a Minister for AI iii) Establish National AI Office iv) Establish an AI Advisory Council v) Teach students to build AI agents
3. Armenia to host the Global AI Action Summit
4. Implement a dedicated National EV Plan
5. Implement a 360-degree foreign policy
6. Deliver a commissioned report into the economic benefits of open borders between Armenia and Turkey (expanded to include jobs and impact on regional areas)
7. Special visa free zone within certain identified areas along Armenia-Turkey border
8. Restore and rebuild the Ani bridge across the Akhurian River, joining Turkey and the city of Ani with Armenia
9. Investment to boost tourism from Iran
10. Secure access to ports of Chabahar and Bandar Abbas in Iran
11. Armenia to be the 'honest broker' between Iran and Western states
12. Establish a trilateral strategic logistics dialogue between Armenia, India and Iran
13. Establish an annual strategic dialogue between Armenia and India Ministers of Foreign Affairs and Defence
14. Recalibrate relations with Russia
15. Lead advocate for the formation of the S20
16. Establish Soft power taskforce
17. Expand shelters for women experiencing domestic violence
18. Appoint Ambassadors to lead a national education awareness campaign to prevent domestic violence

19. Appoint a Minister for Women
20. World Happiness Report – top 50 by 2030 and top 20 by 2050
21. Implement a porcupine defence strategy
22. Government incentives for technology companies that build capabilities that directly benefit Armenia's defence
23. Develop a national intelligence talent pipeline
24. Actively rebuild trust in military service
25. Appoint Special Envoy dedicated to releasing Armenian political prisoners illegally detained in Azerbaijan
26. Enhanced use of data for improved public policy decisions
27. Produce an economic report on the viability of a direct US-Armenia airline route
28. Leverage medical tourism
29. Implement learnings from other successful small nation state investment agencies
30. Grow and expedite Yerevan Metro masterplan
31. Implement additional specific reforms for responsible mining
32. Implement water reforms such as smart meters and drip irrigation
33. Be a skilled negotiator and dealmaker
34. Feasibility study for Citizen based taxation
35. Proactively engage and utilise Armenian diaspora for nation building projects
36. Replace 'Real Armenia' to 'One Armenia' doctrine
37. Be a Smart Nation - Invest in human capital and be a regional hub for digital talent

Endnotes

Chapter One: Silicon Mountain

1. Sassoon Grigorian, *Smart Nation: A Blueprint for Modern Armenia*, Gomidas Institute, 2016

2. Reuters, "Picsart turns unicorn", 27 August 2021, https://www.reuters.com/article/business/picsart-turns-unicorn-with-130-million-funding-led-by-softbank-idUSKBN2FR1IT/

3. Modex, 'Information technology Sector in Armenia', 2 April 2024, https://modex.am/en/information-technology-sector-in-armenia-2023-2/

4. PwC, 'Sizing the prize What's the real value of AI for your business and how can you capitalise?', 2017, https://www.pwc.com/gx/en/issues/analytics/assets/pwc-ai-analysis-sizing-the-prize-report.pdf

5. Modex, 'Armenia lags behind many peers in AI preparedness', 13 January 2025, https://modex.am/en/armenia-lags-behind-many-peers-in-ai-preparedness/#:~:text=Arme-nia%20ranks%2070%20among%20165,%2C%20and%20Azerbaijan%20(0.47)

6. Oxford Insights, 'The Government AI Readiness Index 2024', https://oxfordinsights.com/ai-readiness/ai-readiness-index/

7. Siranush Ghazanchyan, 'Armenia's High-Tech Ministry, French Mistral AI team up to empower the Armenian AI ecosystem', Public Radio of Armenia, 11 February 2025, https://en.armradio.am/2025/02/11/armenias-high-tech-ministry-french-mistral-ai-team-up-to-empower-the-armenian-ai-ecosystem/

8. The Editor, '$500 Million AI Factory To Launch In Armenia By 2026, Powered By NVIDIA, Making it A Regional AI Powerhouse', Zartonk Media, 11 June 2025, https://zartonkmedia.com/2025/06/11/breaking-500-million-ai-factory-to-launch-in-armenia-by-2026-powered-by-nvidia-making-it-a-regional-ai-powerhouse/

9. Zacharie Tazrout, 'Armenia: national artificial intelligence strategy announced to assert itself in the sector', ActuIA, 8 June 2021, https://www.actuia.com/english/armenia-national-artificial-intelligence-strategy-announced-to-assert-itself-in-the-sector/

10. FAST Foundation, 'Generation AI: Educational program', 2022, https://www.fast.foundation/pdf/generation-ai-concept-eng

11. PwC, '2024 AI Jobs barometer', 2024 https://www.pwc.com/gx/en/issues/artificial-intelligence/job-barometer/report.pdf

12. International Energy Agency, 'Armenia', 2022, https://www.iea.org/countries/armenia/energy-mix

13. Daniel Sosa, 'Armenia's energy sector: current developments and challenges', German Economic Team, June 2024, https://www.german-economic-team.com/en/newsletter/armenias-energy-sector-current-developments-and-challenges/

14. International Energy Agency, 'Armenia Energy Profile', March 2023, https://iea.blob.core.windows.net/assets/55834e18-f66e-4642-aed2-7ebff9c54c2c/ArmeniaEnergyProfile.pdf

15. The World Bank, Armenia Energy Fact Sheet 2022, https://armstat.am/file/doc/99544448.pdf

16. Armenia e-mobility Country Profile, 2023, https://asiantransportobservatory.org/documents/66/Armenia_20231015.pdf

17. Ibid.

18. Ruzanna Ayvazyan, 'Developing clean and energy efficient transport sector in Armenia', Government of Armenia, https://www.unescap.org/sites/default/d8files/event-documents/Armenia.pdf

Chapter Two: Smart Foreign Affairs

19. Sassoon Grigorian, *Smart Nation: A Blueprint for Modern Armenia*, Gomidas Institute, 2016.

20. Turkey and Azerbaijan are part of the G20 (twenty largest economies in the world) and D8 respectively. The D8 is the Organisation for Economic Cooperation, established to strengthen ties among developing nations that includes Turkey, Egypt, Nigeria, Pakistan, Iran, Indonesia, Malaysia and Bangladesh. Some of the other groupings that Azerbaijan belong to include the Non Aligned Movement; Organisation of Turkic States, Organisation of Islamic Cooperation; as well as having observer status in OPEC. Russia and Iran are key members of BRICS, which include developing nations, Iran is a member of the Non-Aligned movement and OPEC. Russia is a member of G20 but since the conflict with Ukraine has not been an active participant.

21. Civilnet, 'Interview with Edward Djerejian', 11 June 2024 , https://www.civilnet.am/en/news/781354/why-armenia-needs-a-360-degree-foreign-policy-in-conversation-with-edward-djerejian/

22. JAM News, 'Armenia–Turkey border opens for 10 days - what's next?', 21 March 2025, https://jam-news.net/armenia-turkey-border-opens-for-10-days/

23. Arka News Agency, 'Opening of Armenian-Turkish border can change Armenia's foreign trade structure-Berlin Economics study', 14 September 2023, https://arka.am/en/news/economy/opening_of_armenian_turkish_border_can_change_armenia_s_foreign_trade_structure_berlin_economics_stu/

24. Massis Post, 'Garo Paylan Urges Turkish President to Open Border with Armenia' , 12 August 2025, https://massispost.com/2025/08/garo-paylan-urges-turkish-president-to-open-border-with-armenia/

25. George Conger, 'Turkey to convert historic Armenian cathedral into a mosque', Anglican Ink, 11 July 2025, https://anglican.ink/2025/07/11/turkey-to-convert-historic-armenian-cathedral-into-a-mosque/

26. Ali Alfoneh, 'Iran Will Engage in Countermeasures to Defend Armenia Mashregh News Warns Azerbaijan', Arab Gulf States Institute, 15 September 2022, https://agsiw.org/iran-will-engage-in-countermeasures-to-defend-armenia-mashregh-news-warns-azerbaijan/

27. Seda Hergnyan, 'Armenia Provides 20-30% of Its Energy Needs with Domestic Resources', hetq, 23 May 2023, https://hetq.am/en/article/156089

28. Hovhaness Nazaretyan, 'Armenia's Economic Dependence on Russia: How Deep Does It Go?', EVN Report, 7 July 2023, https://evnreport.com/economy/armenias-economic-dependence-on-russia-how-deep-does-it-go/

29. ArmenPress, 'Meghri free economic zone expected to attract 350-400 million USD investment' 16 March 2017, https://armenpress.am/en/article/882831

30. First Channel News, 'How many people and from which country the most visited Armenia in February?', 11 March 2024, https://www.1lurer.am/en/2024/03/11/How-many-people-and-from-which-country-the-most-visited-Armenia-in-February/1091297

31. Tasnim News, 'Armenia to use Iranian ports for doing business with India', January 2024, https://www.tasnimnews.com/en/news/2024/01/24/3028553/armenia-to-use-iranian-ports-for-doing-business-with-india

32. Dipanjan Roy Chaudhury, 'Armenian Parliament approves loan to build tunnel along Iran border to join initiative', The Economic Times,

5 December 2024, https://economictimes.indiatimes.com/news/international/world-news/armenian-parliament-approves-loan-to-build-tunnel-along-iran-border-to-join-initiative/articleshow/116011488.cms

33. Nesrine Malik, 'The go-between: how Qatar became the global capital of diplomacy', The Guardian, 22 July 2025, https://www.theguardian.com/world/2025/jul/22/how-qatar-became-the-global-capital-of-diplomacy

34. Christine Casimiro, 'Russian Troops to Withdraw From Armenia-Iran Border By 2025', The Defense Post, 11 October 2024, https://thedefensepost.com/2024/10/11/russia-troops-armenia-iran/

35. Alexander Pracht, 'Armenian border guards replace Russians at checkpoint on Turkish border', Civilnet, 3 March 2025, https://www.civilnet.am/en/news/820272/armenian-border-guards-replace-russians-at-checkpoint-on-turkish-border/

36. Tert.am, 'Armenia has no alternative to Russia. Ara Abrahamyan', 26 July 2025, https://tert.am/en/news/2025/07/26/ara-abrahamyan/4238209

37. Hetq, 'Putin Ally Says CSTO Rift May Result in Armenia's Demise', 9 March 2024, https://hetq.am/en/article/164878

38. Hartak, Armenian government, https://hartak.am

39. US Department of State, 'US-Armenia Relations: Fact Sheet', 14 January 2025, https://2021-2025.state.gov/office-of-the-spokesperson/releases/2025/01/u-s-armenia-relations?safe=1

40. Committee of Foreign Relations United State Senate hearing, 14 September 2023, https://www.foreign.senate.gov/imo/media/doc/6667fb89-a975-4fab-d8b8-e8875312e37e/09%2014%2023%20--%20Assessing%20The%20Crisis%20in%20Nagorno-Karabakh.pdf

41. Siranush Ghazanchyan, 'US will provide $11.5 million in humanitarian assistance to the people of Nagorno Karabakh – Samantha Power', Public Radio of Armenia, 26 September 2023, https://en.armradio.am/2023/09/26/us-to-provide-11-5-million-in-humanitarian-assistance-to-the-people-of-nagorno-karabakh-samantha-power-announces-in-armenia/

42. Gabriel Gavin, 'Biden envoy troubled by reports of 'violence against civilians' in Nagorno-Karabakh', Politico, 26 September 2023, https://www.politico.eu/article/joe-biden-samantha-power-nagorno-karabakh-violence-against-civilians-humanitarian-aid-armenia-azerbaijan/

43. The Armenian Mirror-Spectator, 'US Lease of Corridor For Azerbaijan Unacceptable to Armenia', 31 July 2025, https://mirrorspectator.com/2025/07/31/us-lease-of-corridor-for-azerbaijan-unacceptable-to-armenia/

44. US Department of State, 'US-Armenia Relations: Fact Sheet', 14 January 2025, https://2021-2025.state.gov/office-of-the-spokesperson/releases/2025/01/u-s-armenia-relations?safe=1

45. Prime Minister of the Republic of Armenia, 'Memorandum of Understanding between the Government of the United States of America and the Government of the Republic of Armenia regarding an AI and Semiconductor Innovation Partnership', 29 August 2025, https://www.primeminister.am/en/press-release/item/2025/08/29/Nikol-Pashinyan-memorandum-08-08-2025/?fbclid=IwZXh0bgNhZ W0CMTEAAR5cLqjuA9jt-zdOzMZB8ytbY9bJQE8qExqgvUUxfdKjh 62rbfndKH dlJTq_Cg_aem_X7Lp5htOjZSaYxC0h0y6SA

46. https://chinaarmenia.am/en/partners/65/

47. Embassy of Armenia to China, 'Ambassador Vahe Gevorgyan's interview to CGTN', 6 March 2025 https://china.mfa.am/en/news/2025/03/06/amb_CGTN/14033?

48. Suren Sargsyan, 'How Have Chinese-Armenian Relations Evolved?', The Armenian Mirror-Spectator, 30 January 2025, https://mirrorspectator.com/2025/01/30/what-issues-exist-in-armenia-china-relations/

49. Gayane Asryan, 'Soft power: China's spheres of influence in Armenia. Analysis and human stories', JAM News, 25 February 2024, https://jam-news.net/soft-power-chinas-spheres-of-influence-in-armenia-analysis-and-human-stories/

50. Reuters, 'China, Armenia establish strategic partnership', 31 August 2025, https://www.reuters.com/world/china/china-armenia-establish-strategic-partnership-chinese-state-media-report-2025-08-31/?utm_source=chatgpt.com

51. Chair Khana, 'Armenia increases international support for Georgia as Yerevan charts path to West', 12 June 2024, https://chaikhana.media/en/stories/1574/armenia-increases-international-support-for-georgia-as-yerevan-charts-path-to-west

52. Reuters, 'Pashinyan says Armenia, Azerbaijan will not deploy foreign forces on border after peace deal', 13 March 2025, https://

www.reuters.com/world/pashinyan-says-armenia-azerbaijan-will-not-deploy-foreign-forces-border-after-2025-03-13/

53. Sossi Tatikyan, 'EU-Armenia Relations at a Crossroads: Between Normative Values and Pragmatism', EVN Report, 14 May 2025, https://evnreport.com/politics/eu-armenia-relations-at-a-crossroads-between-normative-values-and-pragmatism/

54. Wikipedia, https://en.wikipedia.org/wiki/Armenia%E2%80%93 European_Union_relations

55. Mejlumyan, Ani, 'Armenia gets aid boost from EU' Eurasianet, 15 July 2021, https://eurasianet.org/armenia-gets-aid-boost-from-eu

56. EU Neighbours East, EU announces new €270 million resilience and growth package for Armenia', *EU Neighbours east*. April 5, 2024, https://euneighbourseast.eu/news/latest-news/eu-announces-new-e270-million-resilience-and-growth-package-for-armenia/

57. First Channel News, 'Armenia-EU trade turnover increased significantly last year', 15 March 2024, https://euneighbourseast.eu/news/latest-news/eu-announces-new-e270-million-resilience-and-growth-package-for-armenia/

58. EU Neighbours East, 'Opinion poll shows rising trust for the European Union in Armenia', 15 September 2023, https://euneighbourseast.eu/news/opinion-polls/opinion-poll-shows-rising-trust-for-the-european-union-in-armenia/

59 Marianna Mkrtchyan, 'Poll: over 50% of respondents believe in Armenia's admission to EU in near future', ARM Info, 29 January 2025, https://arminfo.info/full_news.php?id=88727&lang=3

60. Nailia Bagirova, 'Azerbaijani leader sends Karabakh Armenians and Armenia message of cooperation and peace', Reuters, 20 September 2023, https://www.reuters.com/world/azerbaijani-leader-sends-karabakh-armenians-armenia-message-cooperation-peace-2023-09-20/

61. Simon Maghakyan,'Investigation: Armenian Fears of a 'Concentration Camp' in Nagorno-Karabakh May Have Been Warranted', New Lines Magazine, 11 January 2024, https://newlinesmag.com/reportage/investigation-armenian-fears-of-a-concentration-camp-in-nagorno-karabakh-may-have-been-warranted/

62. Armen Sarkissian, The Small States Club, 2023

63. Ibid. p340

64. WIPO, 'The Global Innovation Index 2023', https://www.wipo.int/edocs/pubdocs/en/wipo-pub-2000-2023-section1-en-gii-2023-at-a-glance-global-innovation-index-2023.pdf

65. Oluwatosin Jegede, 'A ranking of the world's most innovative countries in 2023', World Excellence, 11 December 2023, https://www.worldexcellence.com/a-ranking-of-the-worlds-most-innovative-countries-in-2023/

66. International IQ registry, 'Average IQ by country (2025 update)', https://international-iq-test.com/en/test/IQ_by_country

67. PBD Podcast, 'Isarel fighting your war', 26 August 2025, https://www.youtube.com/watch?v=0nsgCE4HC0U

68. Brand Finance, 'Global Soft Power Index 2025', https://static.brandirectory.com/reports/brand-finance-soft-power-index-2025-digital.pdf

69. *MassisPost*, 'Armenian National Philharmonic Orchestra Performs in Persepolis', 6 September 2025, https://massispost.com/2025/09/armenian-national-philharmonic-orchestra-performs-in-persepolis/

70. Harut Sassounian, 'Pashinyan shouldn't have invited Turkish journalists to Yerevan for an interview', *Armenian Weekly*, 18 March 2025, https://armenianweekly.com/2025/03/18/pashinyan-shouldnt-have-invited-turkish-journalists-to-yerevan-for-an-interview/

71. *Zartonk*, 'Armenia's Economy Minister Says $13.3 Million Gained From $6 Million Jennifer Lopez Concert as 15,000 Tourists Attend, Calls for More International Star Performances', 4 August 2025, https://zartonkmedia.com/2025/08/04/armenias-economy-minister-says-13-3-million-gained-from-6-million-jennifer-lopez-concert-as-15000-tourists-attend-calls-for-more-international-star-performances/

Chapter Three: Women and Wellbeing

72. JAM News, 'Three times more domestic violence cases in Armenia last year — Prosecutor General's report', 3 April 2025, https://jam-news.net/three-times-more-domestic-violence-cases-in-armenia-last-year-prosecutor-generals-report/

73. Ibid.

74. United Nations Population Fund, 'Armenia launches first unified digital system for recording domestic violence', 30 January 2025, https://eeca.unfpa.org/en/news/armenia-launches-first-unified-digital-system-recording-domestic-violence

75. Angela Harutyunyan, 'How victims of domestic abuse in Yerevan receive help, revealed through personal stories' JAM News, 14 November 2023, https://jam-news.net/stories-of-abused-women-in-armenia/

76. World Economic Forum, 'Global Gender Gap 2024', June 2024,https://www3.weforum.org/docs/WEF_GGGR_2024.pdf

77. Trading Economic, 'Armenia - Population, Female (% Of Total)' https://tradingeconomics.com/armenia/population-female-percent-of-total-wb-data.html

78. World Happiness Report 2025, https://www.worl ld be around £1500dhappiness.report/

79. Numbeo, 'Current Safety Index by City' https://www.numbeo.com/crime/rankings_current.jsp?displayColumn=1

80. Mark Dovich, 'Pollution, poor waste management among top issues for Yerevan residents in Sunday's election', Civilnet, 18 September 2023 https://www.civilnet.am/en/news/750242/auto-draft/

Chapter Four: The Modern Fortress

81. Jitendra Singh, 'Is Israel's Iron Dome Losing Its Edge? What the Iran Missile Barrage Revealed', SSB Crack News, 18 June 2025, https://news.ssbcrack.com/is-israels-iron-dome-losing-its-edge-what-the-iran-missile-barrage-revealed/

82. International Republican Institute, 'Public Opinion Survey: Residents of Armenia', https://www.iri.org/resources/public-opinion-survey-residents-of-armenia/, October 2024

83. OC Media, Armenia announces 20 percent boost to military spending, 28 September 2024, https://oc-media.org/armenia-announces-20-boost-to-military-spending/

84. Ibid.

85. Arshaluys Barseghyan and Yousef Bardouka, 'Pashinyan says defence spending will not be raised in light of 'established' peace with Azerbaijan', OC Media, 22 August 2025, https://oc-media.org/pashinyan-says-defence-spending-will-not-be-raised-in-light-of-established-peace-with-azerbaijan/

86. Albert Harmon, 'Taiwan's Revolutionary Porcupine Defense Strategy: A Game Changer for Regional Security', Galaxy AI, 13 May 2025, https://galaxy.ai/youtube-summarizer/taiwans-revolutionary-porcupine-defense-strategy-a-game-changer-for-regional-security-a9EmKLkTH8k

87. Wikipedia, https://en.wikipedia.org/wiki/Mossad

88. The Government of Armenia, 'The National Security Strategy of the Republic of Armenia', July 2020, https://www.mfa.am/filemanager/security%20and%20defense/Armenia%202020%20National%20Security%20Strategy.pdf

89. Alexander Pracht, 'Armenia to draft new national security doctrine', Civilnet, 20 February 2025, https://www.civilnet.am/en/news/818568/armenia-to-draft-new-national-security-doctrine/

90. Civilnet, 'Survey shows Armenians concerned over security, trusting in army', 22 July 2025, https://www.civilnet.am/en/news/964707/survey-shows-armenians-concerned-over-security-trusting-in-army/

Chapter Five: Improved Governance

91. Arka News agency, 'Armenia's Anti-Corruption Committee reveals corruption related crimes every week', 2 November 2023, https://arka.am/en/news/society/armenia_s_anti_corruption_committee_reveals_corruption_related_crimes_every_week/

92. Transparency International, Corruptions Perception Index 2024, https://www.transparency.org/en/cpi/2024

93. United Nations, 'e-Government Survey 2024', 2024, https://publicadministration.un.org/egovkb/en-us/Reports/UN-E-Government-Survey-2024

94. Numbeo, 'Cost of Living Index by City 2025 Mid-Year', https://www.numbeo.com/cost-of-living/rankings.jsp

95. Sebastian Staske and Dmitry Chervyakov, 'Relocation of Russian citizens: results from GET surveys', German Economic Team, April 2023, https://www.german-economic-team.com/en/newsletter/relocation-of-russian-citizens-results-from-get-surveys/

96. Maria Zakaryan, 'Imperialism hits the most vulnerable', Chaikhana, 18 July 2023, https://chaikhana.media/en/stories/1490/imperialism-hits-the-most-vulnerable

97. Sebastian Staske and Dmitry Chervyakov, 'Relocation of Russian citizens: results from GET surveys', German Economic Team, April 2023, https://www.german-economic-team.com/en/newsletter/relocation-of-russian-citizens-results-from-get-surveys/

98. Statistical Committee of the Republic of Armenia, https://www.armstat.am/nsdp/

99. European Social Charter, 'Ad hoc report on the cost-of-living crisis submitted by the Government of Armenia', 8 January 2024, https://www.ecoi.net/en/file/local/2110012/ARM_Ad+hoc+report+cost+of+living+2023.pdf

100. Armenpress, '73% of Artsakh's 2021 state budget was provided by Armenia', 31 May 2022, https://armenpress.am/en/article/1084695

Chapter Six: Stimulating Growth – the Next Economic Chapter

101. Arka News agency, 'Number of tourists visiting Armenia in 2024 decreased by 4.7% to 2.2 million people', 5 February 2025, https://arka.am/en/news/society/number-of-tourists-visiting-armenia-in-2024-decreased-by-4-7-to-2-2-million-people/

102. PanARMENIAN.Net, 'Armenia sees 4.6% drop in tourism in 2024', 7 February 2025, https://www.panarmenian.net/eng/news/319142/

103. *Lonely Planet*, 'Best in Travel 2025: The countries Lonely Planet suggests you explore next year', 23 October 2024, https://elpais.com/elviajero/lonely-planet/2024-10-23/best-in-travel-2025-los-paises-que-lonely-planet-propone-descubrir-el-ano-que-viene.html?

104. Emily Lush, 'Why Armenia should be on your radar in 2024', *National Geographic*, 13 June 2024, https://www.nationalgeographic.com/travel/article/paid-content-why-small-but-mighty-armenia-should-be-on-your-agenda-for-2024?

105. Alexander Pracht, 'Yerevan chooses developer to finish Cascade complex', Civilnet, 25 February 2025, https://www.civilnet.am/en/news/819378/yerevan-chooses-developer-to-finish-cascade-complex/

106. The World Bank, 'Armenia tourism and regional infrastructure project' 14 February 2025, https://documents1.worldbank.org/curated/en/099021425162514354/pdf/P504282-026fc0ed-dc6c-4625-b01e-90c079837a6a.pdf

107. Flightconnections.com,   https://www.flightconnections.com/flights-to-armenia-am

108. Arshaluis Mgdesyan, 'Armenia Considering the Possibility of Opening Direct Flights to the US – Deputy Minister', Business Media, 9 September 2024, https://bm.ge/en/news/armenia-considering-the-possibility-of-opening-direct-flights-to-the-us-deputy-minister

109. The Armenia–United States Strategic Partnership Charter is a treaty between Armenia and the United States aimed at strengthening bilateral

relations through cooperation on various issues, including democracy, sovereignty, territorial integrity, and economic and military reforms. The full name of the charter is "Charter on Strategic Partnership between the Republic of Armenia and the United States of America

110. Wikipedia, https://en.wikipedia.org/wiki/Emirates_SkyCargo#cite_note-2

111. Medical Tourism.com, https://www.medicaltourism.com/destinations/armenia#:~:text=Cost%20Comparison&text=Medical%20procedures%20in%20Armenia%20typically,little%20as%20%241%2C000%20in%20Armenia

112. Hranoush Dermoyan, 'Modern Challenges of a Capital City, Part 4: Ongoing Transportation Reforms', EVN Report, 29 November 2024, https://evnreport.com/raw-unfiltered/ongoing-yerevan-transportation-reforms/

Chapter Seven: Smart Management of Natural Resources

113. Dinara Saparova, Florian Hausner, Pavel Bilek, Dmitry Chervyakov , 'Overview of the metals and mining sector in Armenia', German Economic Team, June 2024, https://www.german-economic-team.com/wp-content/uploads/2024/07/GET_ARM_PS_01_2024_EN.pdf

114. EITI, Armenia, https://eiti.org/countries/armenia

115. Gayana Sargsyan, 'Armenia's mining industry: reasons behind its recent highs and lows', JAM news, 15 February 2025,
https://jam-news.net/armenias-mining-industry-reasons-behind-its-recent-highs-and-lows/

116. EITI, Armenia, https://eiti.org/countries/armenia

117. Ani Mejlumyan, 'Renewed clashes at Armenian gold mine highlight government indecision', eurasianet, 11 August 2020, https://eurasianet.org/renewed-clashes-at-armenian-gold-mine-highlight-government-indecision

118. *Times of Israel*, 'Drip Irrigation Helps Save Water Worldwide', 15 May 2014, via Israel Agri https://israelagri.com/drip-irrigation-helps-save-water-worldwide/

119. Max Kaplan-Zantopp, 'How Israel used innovation to beat its water crisis', Israel 21c, 28 April 2022, https://israel21c.org/how-israel-used-innovation-to-beat-its-water-crisis/

Chapter Eight: Tax Reform

120. Michael Levy, 'Bidding farewell to US citizenship: Understanding the exit tax' The Tax Adviser, 1 September 2024, https://www.thetaxadviser.com/issues/2024/sep/bidding-farewell-to-us-citizenship-understanding-the-exit-tax/

121. Josh Summers, 'Income Taxes for Expats in China Explained', China Expat Society, https://www.chinaexpatsociety.com/money/income-taxes-expats-in-china

Chapter Nine: The Art of the Deal

122. Donald Trump, *The Art of the Deal*, Random House, 1987

123. Reuters, 'Pashinyan says Armenia, Azerbaijan will not deploy foreign forces on border after peace deal', 13 March 2025, https://www.reuters.com/world/pashinyan-says-armenia-azerbaijan-will-not-deploy-foreign-forces-border-after-2025-03-13/

124. Prime Minister of the Republic of Armenia, 'Joint Declaration by the President of the Republic of Azerbaijan, the Prime Minister of the Republic of Armenia and the President of the United States of America on the outcomes of their meeting in Washington D.C., United States of America' 9 August 2025, https://www.primeminister.am/en/press-release/item/2025/08/09/Nikol-Pashinyan-visit-US-declaration/

125. Artak Khulian, 'Aliyev Voices Another Demand To Armenia' Azatutyun, 22 July 2024 https://www.azatutyun.am/a/33046074.html

126. *Armenian Weekly*, 'Pashinyan signals readiness to abandon international accountability for Azerbaijan's war crimes' 5 February 2025, https://armenianweekly.com/2025/02/05/pashinyan-signals-read ness-to-abandon-international-accountability-for-azerbaijans-war-crimes/

127. *The Armenian Report*, 'Jared Genser's Step-by-Step Plan for Pashinyan to Free Armenian POWs in Azerbaijan' 4 March 2025, https://www.thearmenianreport.com/post/jared-genser-s-step-by-step-plan-for-pashinyan-to-free-armenian-pows-in-azerbaijan

Chapter Ten: The Diaspora Reimagined

128. World Bank Group, 'The World Bank in Armenia', 2024, https://www.worldbank.org/en/country/armenia/overview

129. Raffi, Elliott, 'The All Armenian Fund: Donors still waiting for the audit', EVN Report, 18 October 2021, https://old.evnreport.com/raw-unfiltered/the-all-armenian-fund-donors-still-waiting-for-the-audit?

130. *Hye Tert*, 'We Must Revisit History of Armenian Genocide, Pashinyan Again Questions the Genocide', 27 January 2025, https://hyetert.org/2025/01/28/we-must-revisit-history-of-armenian-genocide-pashinyan-again-questions-the-genocide/

131. Asbarez staff, 'Pashinyan Says Loss of Artsakh Benefited Armenia', Asbarez, 19 June 2025, https://asbarez.com/pashinyan-says-loss-of-artsakh-benefitted-armenia/

132. Wikipedia, Nikol Pashinyan, https://en.wikipedia.org/wiki/Nikol_Pashinyan?

133. Eric Hagopian, 'Rethinking Armenia and the diaspora', 25 April 2025, Civilnet, https://www.youtube.com/ watch?v=cKBenEQONKU &list=PL1GXE7tjLboJy8ZDZhEpVfxpfm2j-5-xI&index=13

134. Aditya Soni and Deborah Mary Sophia, 'Microsoft to invest $3 billion in India, to expand AI and cloud capacity', Reuters, 7 January 2025, https://www.reuters.com/technology/microsoft-invest-3-bln-expand-azure-ai-capacity-india-2025-01-07/

Chapter Eleven: Trust in Government

135. RadioFreeEurope, 'Armenian Army Chief, Ex-Defense Minister Go On Trial Over Faulty Weapons', 19 January 2022, https://www.rferl.org/a/armania-military-weapons-fraud/31662118.html

136. Bertelsmann Stiftung Transformation, 'BTI 2024 Country Report: Armenia', https://bti-project.org/fileadmin/api/content/en/downloads/reports/country_report_2024_ARM.pdf

137. *Caucasus Research Resource Centre*, 'Caucasus Barometer 2024 Armenia', https://caucasusbarometer.org/en/cb2024am/codebook/

138. *International Republican Institute*, 'Public Opinion Survey: Residents of Armenia', 18 October 2024, https://www.iri.org/resources/public-opinion-survey-residents-of-armenia/

139. *World Population Review*, 'Trust in Government by Country 2025', https://worldpopulationreview.com/country-rankings/trust-in-government-by-country

140. Edelman Trust Institute, '2024 Edelman Trust Barometer Singapore Report', https://www.edelman.com/sites/g/files/aatuss191/files/2024-03/2024%20Edelman%20Trust%20Barometer_Singapore%20Report.pdf

141. Nikol Pashinyan, 'Ideology of real Armenia', 19 February 2025, https://www.primeminister.am/ru/statements-and-messages/item/2025/02/19/Nikol-Pashinyan-Speech/

142. Harut Sassounian, 'Pashinyan falsely blames Armenia's problems on trauma from the 1915 genocide', *Armenian Weekly*, 30 April 2024, https://armenianweekly.com/2024/04/30/pashinyan-falsely-blames-armenias-problems-on-trauma-from-the-1915-genocide/

143. Nikol Pashinyan, 'Implementation of the 2022 State budget', 15 June 2023, https://www.primeminister.am/en/statements-and-messages/item/2023/06/15/Nikol-Pashinyan-Speech/

144. The World Bank Group, 'The Human Capital Index 2020', https://documents1.worldbank.org/curated/en/456901600111156873/pdf/The-Human-Capital-Index-2020-Update-Human-Capital-in-the-Time-of-COVID-19.pdf

145. Statista Research Department, 'Startups in Israel - statistics and facts', Statista, 2025, https://www.statista.com/topics/5024/startups-in-israel/?srsltid=AfmBOoq_sPBmbQxFDijOOHqBwZTY13G-n45MkjJBGP8435vkf2R6Hlr6

PHOTOGRAPHS

1. Armenia's first homegrown unicorn Picsart. Then President of Armenia, Armen Sarkissian visits their offices in 2018 accompanied by founder Hovhannes Avoyan and Michael Vardanian (Source: Office of the Armenian President, https://www.president.am/en/press-release/item/2018/09/07/President-Armen-Sarkissian-visited-PicsArt-office/#gallery-18)

2. The view from ServiceTitan office in Yerevan. The technology sector represents one of the fastest growing sector in the Armenian economy. (Source: LinkedIn/Anush Movsisyan, https://www.civilnet.am/en/news/809334/)

3. Yerevan's vibrant café culture. (Source: Shutterstock) https://www.lonelyplanet.com/articles/top-things-to-do-in-yerevan

4. Yerevan metro, in urgent need for expansion (Source: Tripadvisor, https://www.tripadvisor.com/LocationPhotoDirect Link-g293932-i358602372-Yerevan.html)

5. In a televised address in 2025, Prime Minister Pashinyan espouses the 'Real Armenia' doctrine (Source: Screenshot from Primeminister.am, https://eurasianet.org/armenia-prime-mini ster-promotes-plan-to-radically-transform-society)

6. World's apart, Armenian Prime Minister Nikol Pashinyan with Russian President Vladimir Putin at the Collective Security Treaty Organization (CSTO) in Yerevan, Armenia in 2022. (Source: Reuters, https://www.newsweek.com/armenian-leader-appears-edge-away-putin-leaders-gather-photo-1762136

7. Signing of the declaration of peace presided by US President Trump and Armenia's Prime Minister Pashinyan and Azerbaijan's President Aliyev, 8 August 2025. (Source: Reuters, https://www.reuters.com/world/us/donald-trump/ live-updates-trump-host-azerbaijan-armenia-leaders-white-house-they-sign-peace-2025-08-08/)

8. Yerablur, symbolising the ultimate sacrifice, Armenia's military cemetery located on a hilltop in the outskirts of Yerevan. (Source: Sassoon Grigorian)

9. Armenia's military require a Porcupine defence plan (Source: Armenia's Ministry of Defence)

10. Armenians fleeing their ancestral homeland of Artsakh following Azerbaijan's invasion in September 2023. (Source: Asbarez https://asbarez.com/probe-into-azerbaijans-genocide-of-artsakh-armenians-ongoing-investigative-committee-insists/)

11. Illegally held Artsakh leaders (former Presidents and political leaders) in Baku facing a sham trial. (Source: https://tert.am/en/news/2025/01/27/baku-court/4220955)

12. Armenians celebrating Vardavar, Armenia's water festival 2025, a major tourist drawcard (Source: Sassoon Grigorian)

13. An Armenian water drinking fountain (known as Pulpulak) flowing endlessly in Republic Square Yerevan, embodying Armenia's abundance of this natural resource. (Source: Absolute Armenia https://absolutear menia.com/pulpulak/)

14. The beautiful scenery of Syunik, Armenia's southern region. (Source: Vahe Grigorian)

About the Author

Sassoon Grigorian is a leading government affairs and public policy professional in the technology sector, advising global businesses that have disrupted existing business models.

With more than twenty five years of public policy experience, Sassoon has worked for four Fortune 500 companies, one of the globe's largest public affairs consultancies, and served as a political adviser in Government.

Public policy campaigns initiated by Sassoon have been recipients of several awards including Public Relations and Communication Association (PRCA) Asia Pacific; Information Technology Industry Council (ITI); and The Gold Standard Awards.

Sassoon has served on numerous industry boards and associations, including Armenian community organisations. He holds a Bachelor of Arts (Politics) from Macquarie University and Masters in International Relations from the University of New South Wales.

Sassoon has travelled to Armenia around ten times since 1997 and has three sons.

Smart Nation: A Blueprint for Modern Armenia was first written and published in 2016.

INDEX

www.ingramcontent.com/pod-product-compliance
Lightning Source LLC
Chambersburg PA
CBHW040135270326
41927CB00019B/3392